RELATIONSHIPS EDUCATION
FOR PRIMARY SCHOOLS
(2020)

A PRACTICAL TOOLKIT FOR TEACHERS

RELATIONSHIPS EDUCATION
FOR PRIMARY SCHOOLS
(2020)

A PRACTICAL
TOOLKIT FOR
TEACHERS

Jonathan Glazzard and Samuel Stones

First published in 2020 by Critical Publishing Ltd

British Library Cataloguing in Publication Data
A CIP record for this book is available from the British Library

ISBN: 978-1-913063-61-0

This book is also available in the following e-book formats:

MOBI ISBN: 978-1-913063-62-7
EPUB ISBN: 978-1-913063-63-4
Adobe e-book ISBN: 978-1-913063-64-1

Cover and text design by Out of House Limited
Project Management by Newgen Publishing UK
Printed and bound in the UK by 4edge, Essex

Critical Publishing
3 Connaught Road
St Albans
AL3 5RX

www.criticalpublishing.com

Paper from responsible sources

✚ CONTENTS

+MEET THE AUTHORS

JONATHAN GLAZZARD

SAMUEL STONES

Jonathan Glazzard is Professor of Inclusive Education at Leeds Beckett University. He is series editor for the Positive Mental Health series by Critical Publishing. Jonathan's research explores issues of inclusion, exclusion, marginalisation, disability, sexuality and mental health for children and young people. He is a researcher, teacher educator and author. Jonathan's background is in primary teaching and he is a trustee of several multi-academy trusts.

Samuel Stones is a lecturer, researcher and doctoral scholarship student at Leeds Beckett University. He has co-authored texts for several publishers and has written extensively on inclusion and mental health. Samuel's research explores issues of inclusion, exclusion, marginalisation, sexuality and mental health for children and young people. He is a senior examiner and experienced assessor and also holds a national training role with a large multi-academy trust.

✛ INTRODUCTION

The Department for Education has issued statutory guidance which will make Relationships Education compulsory in all primary schools from September 2020 and Relationships and Sex Education (RSE) compulsory in all secondary schools. Health Education will be compulsory in all schools, except schools in the independent sector. Primary schools will have the option of delivering Sex Education but this is not compulsory.

The statutory guidance has been updated from previous guidance that was issued in 2000 to reflect contemporary families, relationships and legislation. There is an expectation that primary schools teach children different types of relationships including single-parent families, same-sex parents, foster parents and adoptive parents. There is also a requirement to teach young people about online relationships and how to stay safe online. The guidance therefore reflects the reality of life in the twenty-first century.

In primary schools the guidance focuses on the characteristics of positive relationships with specific emphasis on friendships, family relationships and relationships with peers. The curriculum in the guidance is designed to teach children about appropriate ways of treating others, including the need for kindness, consideration, respect, honesty, truthfulness, permission-seeking and personal boundaries. It requires schools to teach children about the features of healthy relationships, including friendships, so that they can identify unhealthy relationships when they encounter them.

Perhaps the most controversial aspect of the guidance is the requirement to teach children about parents who are lesbian, gay, bisexual or transgender (LGBT). The guidance clearly states that children should not experience stigmatisation on the basis of their home circumstances. However, it also states that '*the religious background of all pupils must be taken into account when planning teaching, so that the topics that are included in the core content… are appropriately handled*' (DfE, 2019a, p 12). In addition, the guidance states that '*schools with a religious character may teach the distinctive faith perspective on relationships*' (DfE, 2019a, p 12) and that schools must comply with the Equality Act (2010), under which religion or belief are protected characteristics. The guidance also emphasises the need for '*age appropriate teaching*' (DfE, 2019a, p 8) and advises schools to '*ensure that all of their teaching is sensitive and age appropriate in approach and content*' (DfE, 2019a, p 15).

1

Parental protests outside schools in England featured in media headlines in 2019. The protests were in opposition to a school's LGBT curriculum. The opposition was based on religious arguments. The protests were also replicated across other schools. Opposition to LGBT identities and same-sex relationships serves to highlight the tensions between religion and sexuality/gender. The statutory guidance clearly states that all schools must have a written policy in place that *meets the needs of pupils and parents and reflects the community they serve*' (DfE, 2019a, p 11). The guidance merely stipulates the content that must be taught but does not specify how that content should be taught.

It is clear that schools in some communities will experience greater challenges in implementing aspects of the guidance. Although parents do not have a right to withdraw their children from Relationships Education, there is a need to provide school leaders with clear advice on how to respond to these challenges. The requirement that teaching should be both '*sensitive and age appropriate*' (DfE, 2019a, p 15) is also problematic given that many children live in same-sex relationship families or have family members who identify as LGBT. For these children, LGBT identities and same-sex relationships reflect their lived realities and therefore to omit this from the curriculum of very young children could result in stigmatisation and perpetuate a sense of exclusion. These issues highlight that the implementation of the statutory guidance is not necessarily going to be straightforward and the fact that schools are free to determine how to implement the guidance does not provide reassurance that the framework will be addressed using a consistent approach by all schools.

This book will address these challenges. The structure of the chapters broadly reflects the framework but there are some slight variations. For example, Chapter 2 addresses character education but this is embedded throughout the framework rather than being identified as separate curriculum content. This book also addresses Health Education, which is a mandatory part of the framework.

✚ CHAPTER 1

FAMILIES

CHAPTER OBJECTIVES

After reading this chapter you will understand:

✚ what is meant by the word 'family' within the context of Relationships Education in school;

✚ the key characteristics of healthy family life;

✚ the different types of families and family units;

✚ the legal duties owed by teachers and school staff towards children of LGBT parents;

✚ the role of consultation when addressing parental resistance;

✚ the responsibilities of primary schools in relation to the teaching of marriage;

✚ the characteristics of unhealthy family relationships.

INTRODUCTION

This chapter will introduce you to the word 'family' within the context of Relationships Education. It describes some family units and structures and it outlines the common characteristics that underpin all of these. The chapter also provides several examples of these family units and structures to support you in understanding the concept of family within Relationships Education. Additionally, the chapter outlines the characteristics of healthy family life and the different types of families and family structures that children must be taught about. In doing so, it highlights a range of examples to support your understanding of children's lived realities. We also outline the implications of the statutory guidance in relation to families with LGBT members. In doing so, we highlight the legal responsibility of schools to protect children of LGBT parents from discrimination. The chapter discusses the challenges that schools may face in relation to opposition and it considers the implications of these for faith schools and those with religious character. Some guidance is offered to support schools to address parental resistance and we emphasise the importance of consultation when determining how and when specific content is taught. The chapter also explores the requirement of primary schools to teach children that marriage is available to both opposite-sex and same-sex couples. It provides some discussion in relation to this teaching and offers guidance on 'age appropriate' teaching. The characteristics of unhealthy families and other relationships are also outlined to support your understanding of emotional abuse and neglect.

WHAT IS FAMILY?

Within the context of Relationships Education in school, the word 'family' is used to describe a unit or structure that provides love, security and stability for its members. It might typically include members who are biologically related, although this is not always the case. Some children are raised in family structures where there is no biological relationship between any of the members or some of the members. Families do not have to include children and can vary in size, and marriage does not have to be a feature of family life.

CRITICAL QUESTIONS

+ How would you describe your family structure?
+ Why do you think the statutory guidance emphasises the importance of teaching children about families?
+ How can families support the well-being of their members?

THE CHARACTERISTICS OF HEALTHY FAMILY LIFE

Regardless of the family structure there are specific characteristics associated with healthy families. Healthy families provide their members with love, care, security and stability. Within the context of a healthy family, members demonstrate a commitment to each other, particularly in times of difficulty. They also provide each other with protection and care and they value spending time with each other and sharing each other's lives (DfE, 2019a).

DIFFERENT TYPES OF FAMILIES

Traditional family units which consist of a mother and father who are married and have children are only one type of unit. Within Relationships Education children must be taught about the vast range of family structures that reflect their lived realities. Family forms may include: single parents; LGBT parents; families headed by grandparents, older siblings, aunties or uncles; adoptive parents; foster parents; and carers. This list is not exhaustive.

It is important that your lessons consider the family structures that children in your class belong to. In addition, it is essential that children are not stigmatised on the basis of their home circumstances (DfE, 2019a). Essentially, children need to recognise that families may look different but that healthy families have certain characteristics in common, including the provision of love, care and stability.

FAMILIES WITH LGBT MEMBERS

The statutory guidance states that 'schools should ensure that all of their teaching is sensitive and age appropriate in approach and content' (DfE, 2019a, p 15). Schools must ensure that they comply with the relevant provisions of the Equality Act (2010), given that both sexual orientation and gender reassignment are protected characteristics. Schools therefore have a duty to protect children of LGBT parents from discrimination.

The statutory framework provides schools with the freedom to decide how to teach children about LGBT identities. Although this should be a straightforward aspect to teach, parental protests in 2019 in opposition to the teaching of LGBT content to children in primary schools has illustrated the tensions between sexual orientation, gender identity and religion. The guidance clearly states that 'the religious background of all pupils must be taken into account when planning teaching so that the topics... are appropriately handled' (DfE, 2019a, p 12). In addition, the guidance states that 'schools with a religious character may teach the distinctive faith perspective on relationships, and balanced debate may take place about issues that are seen as contentious' (DfE, 2019a, p 12). The Relationships Education policy must be developed in consultation with parents.

The statutory guidelines raise several questions. These are outlined below.

CRITICAL QUESTIONS

+ If parents object to the teaching of LGBT content, what are the implications for schools in relation to the implementation of the statutory guidance?

+ If schools with a religious character are allowed to teach the distinctive faith perspective on relationships, what are the implications of this?

These are not easy issues for schools to resolve. Section 149 of the Equality Act (2010) places a duty on schools to foster good relations between people who share a protected characteristic and those who do not. This is referred to as the Public Sector Equality Duty. Therefore, regardless of religious perspectives on sexuality and gender identity, schools have a legal duty to promote respect between different groups of people. Primary schools play a crucial role in encouraging children to demonstrate respect for other people, regardless of belief or identity. The teaching of both LGBT identities/relationships and religious perspectives addresses specific fundamental British values, including the need for individual liberty, mutual respect and tolerance of those with different faiths and beliefs.

The starting point for this debate is to understand fundamentally why all children need access to an LGBT curriculum. First, children need to know that LGBT people exist. Many children will already be aware of this because they may have parents, siblings and other family members who identify as LGBT. This raises the question of why it would not be age appropriate to teach LGBT content to very young children when LGBT identities are part of their lived experiences. Second, schools play a critical role in developing inclusive values and attitudes by teaching children that prejudice is not acceptable. Education should create well-rounded individuals who become good citizens. Children need to be taught about treating all people with respect, regardless of their differences. Through challenging prejudice and developing inclusive values and attitudes, schools can therefore advance an agenda for social justice. Third, regardless of personal or religious belief, children need to demonstrate respect towards LGBT people. They will meet LGBT people throughout their education, in the world of work and within their communities. LGBT people exist within all societies and many identify as LGBT and align with a specific religion or belief. These are facts. LGBT identities and relationships may not be acceptable within some religions, but regardless of this, children need to know that not only do LGBT people exist, but within the UK and in other countries, they have a legal right to exist and a legal right to enter into a same-sex relationship. Fourth, teaching children about LGBT identities and relationships addresses, in part, the school's legal duty to meet the provisions of the Equality Act (2010). Fifth, the RSE curriculum in primary schools focuses on relationships rather than sex. Sex Education is not compulsory in primary schools and even if schools choose to offer this, the content will cover the human life cycle, including reproduction. Finally, the RSE curriculum makes no attempt to promote a particular sexual orientation, gender identity or lifestyle.

ADDRESSING PARENTAL RESISTANCE

Following the implementation of the statutory guidance in September 2020, all primary schools must have a policy for Relationships Education that is published on the school website. The law requires primary schools to consult with parents on the development of the policy. Consultation is a process which takes place over time. It provides parents with a formal channel for expressing their views. However, ultimately, it is the responsibility of schools to decide what is taught and how it is taught. Parental resistance to aspects of subject content in Relationships Education should not mean that sensitive topics are not taught. However, schools will need to be sensitive to the views of parents, particularly in relation to *how* subject content is taught rather than *what* is taught. The process of consultation is not to determine *what* it is taught. It is to determine *how* and *when* specific content is taught.

CASE STUDY

LGBT RELATIONSHIPS

YEAR 5, PSHE

A primary school planned to roll out an LGBT curriculum in Year 5. The school wanted the children to learn the vocabulary associated with sexual orientation and gender identity. The curriculum covered a range of terminology, including terms such as gender fluid, non-binary, cisgender and pansexual. The curriculum also covered homophobic, biphobic and transphobic bullying, LGBT history and the celebration of LGBT identities through positive affirmation. In addition, the curriculum covered same-sex marriage. The school was situated in a predominantly Muslim community.

The school developed a consultation process with parents to provide them with a formal channel for expressing their views and concerns. This was not a single event but a process that took place over a period of time. School leaders used this process to introduce parents to the planned curriculum, to listen to their perspectives and to present a rationale to parents to justify the need for the curriculum. The school leaders viewed this process of engagement as a positive step through which a shared set of values could be developed. The aim of the consultation was to give parents a voice, to dispel myths and to strengthen relationships with the parents and community/religious leaders.

Parents of children in Year 5 were initially invited to a briefing event which was led by school leaders. An online questionnaire was also circulated to parents to provide those who could not attend the meeting with an opportunity to have their say about the proposed curriculum. At the meeting, the leadership team initially thanked the parents for attending and explained that this was a process of genuine consultation rather than a tokenistic process. The leaders requested that parents initially listened to the proposals without interrupting the presentation and that there would be an opportunity to ask questions later. The presentation was structured to address the following aspects:

+ the RSE statutory guidance (DfE, 2019a);
+ the Equality Act (2010) and the relevant protected characteristics including religion or belief, sexual orientation and gender reassignment;
+ the implications of the Equality Act (2010) for schools;
+ the fundamental British values and the implications of these for schools;
+ the rationale for the LGBT curriculum;
+ sensitivities in relation to religious views or beliefs;
+ an outline of the proposed curriculum;
+ dispelling myths.

During the presentation leaders emphasised that parents did not have the right to veto the content and did not have a right to withdraw their children from Relationships Education. However, school leaders acknowledged that parents would have conflicting views and reiterated that religious perspectives would be respected. Following the presentation, some of the resources that would be used to support curriculum content were shared with parents. Parents were also given an opportunity to review the unit plan and lesson plans. Governor attendance was required at the meeting to demonstrate governor and trustee support for the planned curriculum.

At the end of the meeting parents were invited to raise questions and concerns. Most of these related to the religious beliefs held by children and parents and the questions demonstrated that the teaching of LGBT content would undermine religious values. This was addressed by explaining to parents that the planned curriculum was not designed to promote a specific sexual orientation, gender identity or lifestyle and that children would be informed that although the religion states that LGBT identities are not recognised, these identities are recognised within the context of British law. This provided a link to fundamental British values.

Parents were invited to comment on how the statutory content in the RSE framework might be addressed. Some parents had specific concerns and were provided with an opportunity to discuss these with school leaders at a separate time. In addition, the consultation questionnaire was circulated to parents, religious leaders and governors to capture a wide range of views. Anonymous responses were not permitted because leaders wanted to follow up specific concerns and questions with individual parents following the completion of the questionnaire. The outcomes of the questionnaire were disseminated across all stakeholder groups.

The school provided an opportunity for leaders, governors, faith leaders and parents to form a working group to develop the curriculum. This demonstrated that the curriculum that was initially presented to parents at the consultation event was a draft curriculum rather than a final curriculum. The working group met for a term to develop the curriculum and the outcomes of this group were disseminated widely. The outcomes included a revised curriculum plan, an information leaflet for parents and a webpage to store the Relationships Education policy, the whole-school curriculum plan for Relationships Education, and a specific section on LGBT related to the unit of work in Year 5. This enabled school leaders to make the content visible to all parents and other stakeholders. The minutes from the consultation events and working group were also placed on the website.

The leadership team addressed specific concerns by arranging meetings with individual parents. Five parents objected to the teaching of LGBT content and decided to hold a protest outside of the school. The school was concerned that this was the beginnings of co-ordinated activity because these parents had started to distribute leaflets to other parents and the leadership team became aware via other parents that closed groups had been created by these five parents on social media. These parents had started to gather outside of school and some staff and children felt intimidated by their presence. It was therefore determined that this was not a peaceful protest. The school leaders responded by requesting a meeting with the organiser. However, it became clear during the meeting that the organiser did not want to engage in constructive dialogue. Following this meeting the protests continued, so the school contacted the police and requested police presence outside the school. This could only be sustained for two days due to lack of police resource and following this the protests continued. The school contacted the local authority who advised the leaders to apply for an injunction to prevent the parents from protesting outside the school.

Following the injunction, the five parents decided to remove their children from the school. There was no further evidence of activism in the local community and specific concerns and questions had been addressed individually with parents. The evidence of the consultation process, including anonymised questionnaire responses, was disseminated to parents and uploaded on the school website. The final LGBT curriculum for children in Year 5 was presented to governors and approved once the consultation had ceased. The curriculum was subsequently implemented and a parent governor was nominated to monitor the implementation.

CRITICAL QUESTIONS

+ When is it 'age appropriate' to teach children about LGBT identities?
+ Why do children need to know about LGBT identities?
+ How can schools work in partnership with parents and community/religious organisations to deliver an LGBT curriculum?

CASE STUDY

DIFFERENT TYPES OF FAMILY

YEAR 2, PSHE

Children in Year 2 were learning about different types of families. Alex, the teacher, wanted the children to understand that there are different types of families. He wanted them to learn that some children have two dads, others have two mums and some children have a mum and a dad. He wanted them to learn that some children are born into families where there is only one parent – either a mum or a dad – and some children are fostered and others are adopted. Alex was keen to represent all the different types of family types of the children in his class.

He started the lesson by asking the children to explain what they understood by the word 'family'. He asked them to discuss with their talk partner the people in their own family. He then showed the children the Stonewall resource which shows a variety of different family structures. You can access this resource using this link: www.stonewall.org.uk/system/files/poster_different_families.pdf (accessed 30 January 2020).

Alex outlined the different types of families using the Stonewall poster. He explained that although families may look different, healthy families share certain characteristics. He asked the children to identify what families had in common and he wrote their ideas on the board. The children knew that families provide love and care for each other. Through effective questioning, Alex developed the children's understanding by asking them to draw on their own experiences of family life. Through this the children developed an understanding that healthy families provide protection, financial support, food, clothing and shelter.

On each table there was a copy of this resource and Alex asked the children to locate their family type on the poster and to identify other families that they knew, matching these to the families on the poster. Alex then asked the children how people within families can demonstrate their love for each other. The children identified specific actions including listening to one another, providing hugs and spending time together. Some children said that giving each other gifts on special occasions was also another way of demonstrating love. Alex acknowledged this but then asked the children to identify which was more important, providing gifts or spending time with one another.

Alex then asked the children to work in pairs. He gave them a set of cards with the following statements on, which they had to order from least important to most important:

+ providing gifts;

+ spending time with one another;

+ giving each other money;

+ providing food and shelter;

+ doing exciting things together;

+ protecting one another.

Following this task Alex collected some feedback and the class as a whole decided on how to order the cards. He modelled this on the board.

Alex then asked the class to work in groups. A copy of the Stonewall poster was displayed on each table and the children were asked to use the poster to identify their own family structure and share this with the group. He then gave each group a set of cards, two sorting hoops and two labels: healthy families and unhealthy families. Alex asked the children to read the statements and as a group to decide whether the statement needed to be assigned to the healthy family hoop or the unhealthy family group. Statements included:

+ loving each other;

+ caring for each other;

+ spending time together;

+ not spending time together;

+ families in which people do not respect each other;

+ shouting at each other;

+ making each other happy;

+ making each other sad;

+ spending all the family time using technology.

Alex also included some statements which he anticipated would be assigned to the 'unhealthy families' category. These included:

+ not providing enough money;

+ not providing enough food;

+ not providing new clothes;

+ not providing expensive gifts.

Some of the children automatically associated these characteristics with unhealthy families. At this stage of the lesson Alex noticed that one child, Sophie, was upset. Alex went over to talk to Sophie to ascertain what the problem was. Sophie told Alex that another child in the group had made an unkind comment about Sophie's family. Sophie's parents did not have a lot of money and could not afford to buy her expensive gifts and new clothes. In fact, many of her clothes were second-hand. The other child made an insensitive comment to Sophie, which resulted in Sophie becoming distressed. Alex immediately and calmly intervened and spoke to the group about this because other children had over-heard the comment. He explained that these factors were not a characteristic of unhealthy families and he also explained that Sophie's family circumstances were private. Alex explained that some families may have a lot of money but if the individuals within the family did not show love, care and respect to other members of their family then this was not healthy. He went on to explain that families may not have a lot of money but family members can still show love, care and respect.

Following the task Alex modelled the task on the board. Through discussion and skilled questioning Alex helped the children to understand that lack of finances does not make families unhealthy and that the most important features of family life were love, care, respect and protection towards other members of the family. This was a critical teaching point in the lesson because it enabled many children to reframe their understanding.

During the last stage of the lesson, Alex asked the children to identify their own contribution to making their family healthy. This was an interesting question because some of the children did not realise that their own actions might affect the characteristics of family life. He then asked the children to complete a concept map on which they were required to identify their own contribution to their families.

MARRIAGE

Primary schools are required to teach children that marriage is available to both opposite-sex and same-sex couples in England and Wales. The Marriage Act (2013) extended marriage to same-sex couples and the ceremony may be a civil or religious ceremony. Children need to be taught that marriage represents a formal and legally recognised commitment of two people to each other and that this commitment is intended to be lifelong (DfE, 2019a). Schools will therefore need to decide when to introduce same-sex marriage. However, it should be recognised that children may have same-sex parents who are married. This therefore raises a question about 'age appropriate' teaching. Given that very young children might have same-sex parents who are married, it could be argued that same-sex marriage should be taught at the start of the Relationships Education curriculum to reflect the lives that children live.

UNHEALTHY FAMILIES AND OTHER RELATIONSHIPS

Children need to understand the characteristics of unhealthy family relationships which make them feel unhappy or unsafe. These relationships usually involve an abuse of power where children are subjected to excessive forms of control where they may experience various forms of abuse. This also includes subjecting children to emotional abuse and neglect. The curriculum should be designed to teach children how to seek help or advice from others if it is needed.

SUMMARY

This chapter has considered the word 'family' within the context of Relationships Education. It has explained family units and structures and the common characteristics of these. The chapter has also outlined the characteristics of healthy family life and the different types of families and family structures that children must be taught about. The chapter has outlined the responsibilities of schools in relation to families with LGBT members and it has acknowledged the challenges that schools may face in relation to opposition. There has also been a consideration of these challenges within the context of faith schools and those with religious character. Guidance has been offered to support schools to address parental resistance and we have emphasised the importance of consultation to support the determination of how and when specific content is taught. We have highlighted the requirement of primary schools to teach children that marriage is available to both opposite-sex and same-sex couples. Some guidance on 'age appropriate' teaching has been offered to support your understanding of the statutory guidance. The characteristics of unhealthy families and other relationships have also been outlined.

FURTHER READING OR SOURCES OF FURTHER INFORMATION

Department for Education (DfE) (2019) *Parental Engagement on Relationships Education*. London: DfE. [online] Available at: https://assets.publishing. service.gov.uk/government/uploads/system/uploads/attachment_data/file/ 836503/6.5987_DfE_Consult-Paper_Relationships-Parental_A4-P_Op4_v7_ weba.pdf (accessed 30 January 2020).

Department for Education (DfE) (2019) *Understanding Relationships and Health Education in Your Child's Primary School: A Guide for Parents*. London: DfE. [online] Available at https://assets.publishing.service.gov.uk/ government/uploads/system/uploads/attachment_data/file/812593/RSE_ primary_schools_guide_for_parents.pdf (accessed 30 January 2020).

+ CHAPTER 2
CHARACTER

CHAPTER OBJECTIVES

After reading this chapter you will understand:

+ the aims of character education;

+ the importance of adopting a whole-school approach to character education;

+ key considerations in relation to the planning and delivery of character education;

+ the importance of culture, behaviour, resilience and confidence;

+ how co-curriculum and volunteering opportunities can contribute to character education;

+ how to promote equality of opportunity within the delivery of character education.

INTRODUCTION

This chapter introduces the concept of character education and emphasises the importance of values, attitudes, skills and behaviours. It also considers the implications of character education within the context of school responsibilities. Additionally, the chapter provides guidance in relation to the key challenges that schools are likely to experience with their planning and delivery of character education. There is some discussion on the importance of character education and this is situated within the requirements of the statutory guidance. The chapter also considers character education in relation to positive school culture and the role of the leadership team is outlined. Some guidance is provided to support schools to develop learners' resilience and confidence and we emphasise the importance of co-curriculum and volunteering opportunities. Finally, the chapter emphasises the role that schools play in promoting equality of opportunity and some guidance is provided to support teachers and school staff.

WHAT IS CHARACTER EDUCATION?

Character education aims to develop a set of values, attitudes, skills and behaviours that support personal development and contribute to positive long-term outcomes (Walker et al, 2017). Character education aims to support children to develop moral and civic values. This enables them to understand the difference between right and wrong and to understand their responsibilities as citizens to the local and global communities in which they live.

There is no correct approach to delivering character education in schools. However, it is important that school leadership teams view the development of character as being central to the culture, values and vision of the school (Walker et al, 2017). It is also important to adopt a whole-school approach (Walker et al, 2017). This ensures that specific character virtues are consistently reinforced in all classrooms. It is also important that teachers and leaders exemplify the character virtues that they want children to develop (Walker et al, 2017). This has implications for the way in which adults speak to children.

Some children live their lives surrounded by adults in their families and in the wider community who do not demonstrate positive character virtues. It is important to be aware that the values that the school seeks to promote may be in direct conflict with the values that are consistently

17

demonstrated in homes and communities. In this case, children may have to reframe their character traits when they are in the context of the school. Some children will internalise the positive character virtues that the school promotes, and these will shape their identities as they develop. Others will learn to 'switch' the positive character virtues on when they are in school even though they may adopt a different set of virtues when they are outside the school. The key challenge for schools is therefore how to address the dissonance between the character virtues that are promoted outside of school and those that are promoted within schools. More significantly, however, is how schools support children to internalise the positive character virtues that are essential to long-term success so that they consistently demonstrate them, believe in them and subsequently reject the negative character virtues that they are exposed to outside of school.

CRITICAL QUESTIONS

+ How might social and cultural contexts influence the development of character?
+ Why do you think that character education has become a policy priority?

THE IMPORTANCE OF CHARACTER

Although character education is not identified as a separate strand within the statutory guidance (DfE, 2019a), it is embedded within specific themes. Within 'caring friendships', specific character traits are addressed. Character traits include respect, motivation, emotional and social regulation, social confidence, social and communication skills, trustworthiness, resilience, leadership, loyalty, kindness, courtesy, truthfulness, courage and generosity. Within 'respectful relationships', courtesy and manners are identified as key character traits. Character education is therefore part of Relationships Education in primary schools. The statutory guidance states:

A growing ability to form strong and positive relationships with others depends on the deliberate cultivation of character traits and positive personal attributes (sometimes referred to as "virtues") in the individual.

(DfE, 2019a, p 20).

Evidence suggests that character education supports the development of a positive school culture, leads to a more conducive learning environment and leads to improved behaviour and attendance and motivation (OECD, 2015; Walker et al, 2017). It also leads to positive long-term outcomes including facilitating access to higher education (Walker et al, 2017) and promotes good mental well-being (DfE, 2019b; Taylor et al, 2017). Character education drives equality and social mobility (Chanfreau et al, 2016). Research has found that specific character traits are associated with positive outcomes. These are summarised below:

+ *High self-efficacy is associated with better performance and greater persistence and motivation. Self-efficacy is a prerequisite investing sustained effort in a task.*

+ *High levels of intrinsic motivation are associated with greater persistence and achievement.*

+ *Good self-regulation, including the ability to delay gratification, is associated with greater attainment.*

+ *High levels of resilience are associated with greater well-being.*

+ *Mindsets are malleable and supporting children to develop a growth mindset may result in small to medium size improvements in later performance.*

(Gutman and Schoon, 2013)

Character is a complex concept and multifaceted. Important aspects include:

+ *the ability to stay motivated by long-term goals, including the ability to invest effort and persevere with something despite setbacks;*

+ *the development of moral attributes or virtues;*

+ *the acquisition of social confidence, including the ability to make persuasive arguments, listen to others and demonstrate good manners and courtesy toward others;*

+ *the ability to appreciate the importance of long-term commitments, for example by demonstrating commitment to a relationship, a vocation, a faith or world view or a commitment to the local community.*

(DfE, 2019b)

The *Education Inspection Framework* (Ofsted, 2019) embeds character education within the strand of 'personal development'. Inspectors will evaluate the curriculum and the school's work in supporting learners to develop their character, including their resilience, confidence and independence.

CRITICAL QUESTIONS

+ What character virtues are important to you?
+ What factors shaped the development of your own character?

Research demonstrates that children who are focused on intrinsic-related goals for engaging in an activity show greater motivation, more persistence and higher achievement compared to children who are focused on extrinsic-related goals (Gutman and Schoon, 2013). Studies have shown that the ability to self regulate is a significant predictor of attainment (Moffitt et al, 2011). There is also evidence that teaching children to develop appropriate social behaviour improves attainment (Durlak et al, 2011).

DEVELOPING A POSITIVE SCHOOL CULTURE

School leaders are responsible for creating the school ethos and culture. The school ethos should embody a strong vision for character and personal development (DfE, 2019b). The importance of positive virtues and character traits should be embodied within the vision. These might include resilience, self regulation, social behaviours and virtues. An effective school leadership team will foster a sense of pride, belonging and identity among all members of the school community.

DEVELOPING POSITIVE BEHAVIOUR

Research suggests that childhood self-control predicts achievement and adjustment outcomes, even in adulthood (Gutman and Schoon, 2013). Good behaviour is an essential characteristic of effective schools. It creates the conditions for effective learning and it prepares children for life after leaving school. Good discipline also ensures that schools are safe places for all members of the school community.

An essential aspect of character education is to promote positive social behaviours so that children can learn effectively and are well prepared for adult life.

Children should be taught about the importance of demonstrating respect towards others, regardless of any differences. Demonstrating respect is a fundamental characteristic of an inclusive society. Teaching children about good manners and courtesy ensures that they can conduct themselves appropriately within educational, social and workplace contexts. This is particularly important in cases where children do not live in families or communities where these virtues are demonstrated.

DEVELOPING RESILIENCE AND CONFIDENCE

Children who demonstrate resilience can recover from adverse situations and this can support them in achieving goals. However, the concept of resilience is problematic because resilience is relational. What this means is that a person's ability to be resilient is influenced by their relationships with others. Children are more likely to have greater resilience if they have access to social support networks that can offer emotional and practical support during challenging times. Access to supportive teachers, peers, family and community support can enable individuals to be resilient during times when they experience adversity. In addition, resilience is also contextual. Resilience varies from one context to another and it is therefore possible to demonstrate greater resilience in some contexts than it is in others.

The same also applies to confidence. An individual's confidence can vary across social, academic and other domains and it can vary between different contexts. It is also influenced by one's self worth and self efficacy. Self efficacy is an individual's appraisal of their own competences within specific domains, whereas self worth is an individual's overall view of themselves based on evaluations that others (peers, family, teachers) have made on them. Both self efficacy and self worth contribute to overall self esteem. It is possible for both aspects to be high or low or for one to be high and the other to be low. Overall, self esteem affects confidence.

The good news is that resilience and confidence are dynamic traits and can be altered. Supportive school environments can buffer against the effects of negative environments within homes and communities which detrimentally impact on both resilience and confidence.

Children can be taught to develop their resilience, for example, by teaching them to recover from 'failure' or teaching them to be resilient to feedback. Exposure to teachers who empower children can dramatically improve a person's confidence. In addition, the experience of academic success is a vital ingredient for improving confidence. As children begin to realise that they are capable of achieving, their self efficacy starts to improve and this increases their self esteem and confidence. Children can be taught to demonstrate social confidence in specific situations, even if they do not feel confident. They can be taught how to appear confident but more importantly a skilled teacher can provide children with genuine confidence by getting them to believe in themselves.

Access to a well-designed curriculum helps children to develop confidence. Knowledge and skills should be sequenced correctly. This enables children to make sense of new subject content because correct sequencing provides them with the foundational knowledge and skills upon which new content can be accommodated. In addition, access to a broad and rich curriculum that provides children with cultural capital is essential for developing social confidence and social mobility. One way of achieving this is to develop their vocabulary and knowledge so that children from all social backgrounds can experience and benefit from the same opportunities.

DEVELOPING THE CO-CURRICULUM

As part of the character education curriculum, schools should ensure that there is strong provision for co-curricular activities. A well-planned co-curriculum can build social confidence and self esteem and improve motivation, attendance and academic outcomes for children (DfE, 2019b). Research demonstrates that participation in outdoor adventure programmes has positive effects on the psychological, behavioural, physical and academic outcomes of young people (Gutman and Schoon, 2013).

Activities may include access to sporting or other physical activities, performance, the arts, volunteering, debating, cooking and participation in service. This is not an exhaustive list. The critical point is that schools should ensure that all pupils can participate in the co-curriculum, including those pupils who are the most disadvantaged. Barriers to participation may include the direct costs of activities and to address this, schools should subsidise activities to prevent financial constraints becoming a barrier to equal opportunities. The co-curriculum should be designed to enable young people to compete and perform. These opportunities improve social confidence and self esteem.

CASE STUDY

COMMUNITY PARTICIPATION

YEAR 2, DESIGN AND TECHNOLOGY

A primary school strengthened its links with the local community to provide opportunities for pupils to support cooking events at local food markets. The school's senior leaders asked local businesses and farmers to support the community initiative. This enabled the school to remove barriers to participation and ensure that all pupils were able to participate. Pupils were able to use dedicated curriculum time to cook and bake and prepare produce for the local food markets. The school also had a working farm and pupils were also able to support the feeding of livestock and the collection and harvesting of crops. The local food markets offered opportunities for pupils to compete and showcase their work to residents. The school committed existing funds to enable pupils to travel to and from local competitions and events. This project supported pupils to improve their social confidence and self esteem while also increasing attendance and motivation. The school's senior leaders reviewed the project after one year and decided to expand their current provision by inviting other schools to participate. This provided further opportunities for collaboration between local schools and employers as well as with those in the wider community.

DEVELOPING AND PROMOTING THE VALUE OF VOLUNTEERING

Volunteering empowers children by enabling them to make a positive contribution to their local community. It helps children to develop a civic mindset and provides them with an opportunity to engage in meaningful work. Children can participate in a range of volunteering opportunities. These may include fundraising activities for local and national organisations, protecting the environment and providing services to elderly people in the local community. Research findings suggest that volunteering produces moderate effects for academic outcomes and small effects for non-cognitive outcomes including social skills, self perceptions, and motivation (Gutman and Schoon, 2013).

CASE STUDY

VOLUNTEERING

YEAR 5, PSHE

The headteacher of a primary school recognised the value of volunteering opportunities and decided to prioritise this aspect of school provision for all pupils across the school. The headteacher dedicated existing training time to provide an opportunity for teachers and school staff to discuss how volunteering opportunities could be provided for all pupils. The staff worked together to identify the local charities that may have been able to benefit through the formation of a working partnership with the school. These included charities dedicated to animal welfare, environmental sustainability and social welfare and health as well as humanitarian aid. Over several weeks the parents in the School Committee group contacted these charities to build partnerships and establish whether there were opportunities for pupils to support charitable work. Pupils were able to attend placements and engage with local charity groups and many of these charities also visited the school to further strengthen existing relationships. In a pupil voice activity, pupils reported increased levels of motivation as a result of their charitable work.

DEVELOPING EQUALITY OF OPPORTUNITY

School leadership teams need to identify the barriers to participation in relation to some of the activities outlined in this chapter. Barriers could include the cost and timing of activities, lack of parental support and lack of confidence in children. Leadership teams should consider how these barriers will be addressed so that children from all backgrounds have opportunities to participate, particularly in the co-curriculum. The co-curriculum provides children from the most disadvantaged backgrounds with cultural capital by developing a broader range of interests, knowledge and skills. Access to a co-curriculum and volunteering improves social confidence and self esteem, which contribute to social mobility.

SUMMARY

This chapter has introduced the concept of character education and it has outlined the responsibility of schools in relation to the promotion of values, attitudes, skills and behaviours. It has also considered the implications of character education within the context of school responsibilities and statutory guidance. Guidance has been provided to support schools with the challenges that they may face with the planning and delivery of character education. There has also been some discussion on the importance of character education and we have considered character education in relation to positive school culture and the role of the leadership team. Some case study material has been offered to support your reflection of existing practice and we have encouraged you to consider the benefits of co-curriculum and volunteering. The chapter has also outlined how teachers and school staff can promote equality of opportunity.

FURTHER READING OR SOURCES OF FURTHER INFORMATION

Association for Character Education (nd) Latest News. [online] Available at: www.character-education.org.uk (accessed 4 February 2020).

Girlguiding (nd) With Girlguiding Girls Have the Best Experiences. [online] Available at: www.girlguiding.org.uk (accessed 4 February 2020).

PSHE Association (nd) Resources and Curriculum Home. [online] Available at: www.pshe-association.org.uk/curriculum-and-resources (accessed 4 February 2020).

Scouts (nd) Help Inspire the Doers and Give it a Goers of the Future. [online] Available at: www.scouts.org.uk/home (accessed 4 February 2020).

+CHAPTER 3

CARING RELATIONSHIPS

CHAPTER OBJECTIVES

After reading this chapter you will understand:

+ the importance of friendships and the characteristics of caring friendships;

+ the challenges that may be experienced within friendship groups;

+ the importance of recognising unhealthy friendships and being able to seek support.

INTRODUCTION

This chapter emphasises the importance of friendships in relation to an individual's emotional well-being. It also highlights the responsibilities placed upon schools to teach children about how to establish and develop friendships. Additionally, the chapter outlines the differences between online and offline relationships and it provides some key considerations in relation to these to support your reflection. The characteristics of caring relationships are provided and some practical guidance is offered with a case study to illuminate effective practice. Some of the challenges associated with friendships are identified and these are summarised within the context of school responsibilities and the statutory framework. Finally, the chapter explains the importance of children being taught how to recognise unhealthy friendships and how to seek additional support in these situations.

THE IMPORTANCE OF FRIENDSHIPS

Friendships are important for many reasons. Healthy friendships help us to feel happy and secure and are therefore important to our emotional well-being. The statutory framework (DfE, 2019a) requires primary school children to understand the importance of friendships and the characteristics of healthy friendships. Children need to understand that they can choose who to establish friendships with, unlike the relationships that they have with their families. In addition, children need to be taught how to develop friendships. Friendships can exist in both the online and offline worlds. Fundamentally, children need to understand that friendships that are established in the online world may be different to those friendships they establish in the offline world. Friendships can develop with people of any age, although they are likely to develop between people of similar age due to shared interests. However, children need to understand the risks associated with establishing friendships with people who are much older, particularly when these are established through social media. Friendships with older people may also be established through family connections. However, children need to understand that this does not guarantee that the friendship is healthy. Children should be taught to recognise when a friendship may be unhealthy and they should know how to access support in these circumstances.

THE CHARACTERISTICS OF CARING FRIENDSHIPS

The characteristics of healthy friendships include mutual respect, truthfulness, trust, loyalty, kindness, generosity, shared interests and experiences and the provision of support during challenging times. Healthy friendships are positive and welcoming towards others, and do not make others feel lonely or excluded (DfE, 2019a).

CASE STUDY

HEALTHY FRIENDSHIPS

YEAR 2, PSHE

This series of 12 lessons will explore the characteristics of healthy friendships. Two lessons will be allocated to each characteristic. In total, six characteristics will be addressed over 12 lessons. The unit will cover the following characteristics: truthfulness, respect, trust, loyalty, kindness and generosity. The outline plans for two lessons on 'truthfulness' are given below.

Lesson 1

+ Explain to the children that they will learn about 'truthfulness'. Ask them to suggest what this word might mean. Ask them to give examples of when they have told the truth or not told the truth.

+ Read the story of *The True Story of the Three Little Pigs* by Jon Scieszka or play the video (www.youtube.com/watch?v=I45MxOOLb7k, accessed 30 January 2020). This story presents the Wolf's account of the story.

+ Following the story use *community of enquiry* as a pedagogical approach. This teaching strategy is based on the effective use of questioning to promote higher order thinking. The children can be seated in a circle for this activity. Through questioning, children develop their own reasoned responses to the text. In relation to this story questions might include:

- Do you think the Wolf was telling the truth?
- What evidence is there in the text that suggests the Wolf was lying?
- What was his motive?
- Did the Pigs believe him when he said he wanted to borrow a cup of sugar?
- What evidence is there in the text that shows that the Pigs did not believe him?
- Was the Wolf a friend to the Pigs? How do you know?
- Why do you think he told this story?

Lesson 2

✚ Ask the children if they can remember what they are learning about. Remind them that they are learning about 'truthfulness'.

✚ Recap on the key events of the story. Use a washing line and key illustrations from the story and ask the children to sequence the illustrations on the washing line.

✚ On tables a sorting activity will be prepared. The children will be given scenarios which illustrate examples of friends either being truthful or telling lies. There will two sorting hoops on the table: one labelled 'truthful' and the other labelled 'not truthful'. Ask the children to work together to read each of the scenarios and to sort them into the correct sorting hoop. Include some 'red herrings' to promote higher order thinking, for example:

Amy and Sanna were friends. Sanna had woken up late and had not had time to brush her hair. Sanna's hair looked a mess. Sanna asked Amy if she looked okay and Amy said she looked fantastic.

✚ In this example Amy is clearly not telling the truth but she makes this choice to protect Sanna's feelings so this might be an example of a situation where it is acceptable not to tell the truth.

✚ Carry out a circle time activity. Ask the children to share examples of when they told the truth to a friend. Repeat this by asking them to share examples of when they did not tell the truth to a friend and ask them to explain how this made them feel. Repeat the activity again by asking the children to share an example of when a friend demonstrated truthfulness towards them.

+ Repeat this lesson structure with each of the other five characteristics of healthy friendships. Vary the final two lessons by including the following activities:

+ Synonym activity
  − Print the following cards on blue paper: respect, truthfulness, trust, loyalty, kindness, generosity.
  − Print synonyms for each of these words on yellow paper, for example: loyalty − faithfulness, devotion; generosity − kindness, unselfish, hospitable.
  − Ask the children to match the yellow cards with the correct blue card. The aim of this activity is to develop children's vocabulary, thus providing them with cultural capital.

+ Provide the children with cards that include words to denote the characteristics of healthy and unhealthy friendships. Words might include loyal, respect, trusting, kindness, generous, truthful, nasty, spiteful, unkind, etc. Ask the children to sort the words into two sorting hoops − healthy friendships and unhealthy friendships.

+ Provide the children with scenarios which describe either healthy or unhealthy friendships and ask them to sort them into sorting hoops and justify their responses.

Throughout this unit it is important to identify possible misconceptions and address these within the appropriate lesson. For example, children might associate generosity with the act of giving money, food or other gifts to friends. Although these can be examples of generosity, it is important to also emphasise to children that giving time, kindness, love and support to friends are also examples of generosity. It is also important that children understand that although acts of generosity are usually motivated by kindness, sometimes people may use generosity to manipulate friendships. You will need to give the children good examples of this to support their understanding.

CRITICAL QUESTIONS

+ Children observe friendships between adults within their homes and communities. What impact might this have on their understanding of behaviours within friendships?

+ How might you support a child who has been subjected to unhealthy friendships?

THE CHALLENGES WITHIN FRIENDSHIPS

The statutory framework (DfE, 2019a) requires children to understand that challenges can occur within friendships. It is natural for people to 'fall out' within friendships. This usually happens because friends care about each other and someone within the friendship group may have done or said something which has intentionally or unintentionally hurt someone else's feelings. If we did not care about our friends then we would not get upset by things that they say or do to us. Children need to understand that if friendships are special to us then it is important to work through these challenging situations to repair the friendship. Working through challenges within friendships can sometimes not only repair a friendship, but also strengthen it. Children need to understand that resorting to violence is never right.

CRITICAL QUESTIONS

+ What challenges have you experienced within your friendships?

+ How have you resolved these challenges?

CASE STUDY

REPAIRING FRIENDSHIPS

YEAR 6, ENGLISH

This case study introduces children in Year 6 to the challenges that they may encounter within friendships.

Introduce the class to the following scenario:

You have told one of your closest friends one of your deepest secrets. It is a secret that you have kept for a long time. It is something that has worried you and you have wanted to tell someone but you needed to be sure that you could trust someone before disclosing the secret. Your friend listened to your secret and promised to keep the secret. However, a few days later, to your horror, you find out that your friend has shared your secret with other people, including some of your other friends.

This is a unit of work which spans four lessons. The following description provides an outline of the lessons. The lessons are taught within the subject of English using drama.

Lesson 1

+ Inform the children that they are learning about breach of trust within friendships.

+ Ask the children to think about what the secret might be. Ask them to think about whether they have any secrets that they want to share with their friends but are too frightened to disclose them.

+ Introduce the strategy of *tableaux:* Ask them to take on the role of the person who has held the secret. Ask them to imagine how they might feel at the point when they realise that their secret has been shared. They might feel embarrassed, frightened or angry and they might experience other emotions. Ask them to think about what their facial expressions and body posture might look like at the time when they realise that their secret has been disclosed. Ask them to stand in a space and to rehearse the facial expression and body posture. Tell the class that when you count down from five to zero you want them to perform a frozen image that represents their facial expression and body posture. Give them a short time to rehearse this. Then count down from five to zero and ask them to hold a still body image as though you are taking a photograph to represent their emotions at that time. Rehearse this several times to get a near-perfect frozen image.

+ Next, introduce the strategy of *thought-tracking*. The children will, once again, be asked to perform the tableaux that they have just rehearsed. Inform them that you will count down from five to zero and when you reach zero the children will move into the frozen image. Explain that you will, at this point, walk around the room and touch their shoulder. When you touch their shoulder, they will be expected to say a word or short phrase that best illustrates how they are feeling when they discover that their friend has broken the trust that they thought they had. Give them two or three minutes to think through what they will say when you touch their shoulder. Then ask them to move into their tableaux. Move around the room and select specific children to articulate how they are feeling.

Lesson 2

+ Remind the children that they are learning about breach of trust within friendships.

+ Recap with the children about the scenario that was introduced in the previous lesson and ask them to explain how they might feel if their friend had disclosed one of their secrets.

+ Introduce the strategy of *paired improvisation* in drama. Place them in pairs and ask one of them to take on the role of the person who holds the secret and the other to take on the role of the person who has 'spread' the secret to other people. Tell them that they are going to perform an improvisation in which they will talk the situation through together. This is not a scripted conversation. The children will need to improvise the conversation. You may need to model the strategy yourself either with a child or with a teaching assistant before you ask them to practise the improvisation.

+ First ask each pair to decide what the secret is.

+ The conversation will be structured loosely as follows:
  − You: *I told you my secret because... Why did you tell other people?*
  − Friend: *I told other people because...*
  − You: *This is how it made me feel...*
  − Friend: *After I had told people this is how I felt...*
  − You: *Can I trust you again?*
  − Friend: *Yes, you can trust me because...*

+ Give them 5–10 minutes to practise their paired improvisations. Some children may need a 'talking frame', which supports them in structuring the conversation. This could include an outline of the different aspects of the conservation on a sheet for them to follow and sentence openers/starters.

+ Ask each pair to perform their improvisations to the rest of the class.

Lesson 3

+ Remind the children that they are learning about breach of trust within friendships.

+ Recap what they did in lesson 2.

+ Introduce the strategy of *conscience alley:* divide the class into two groups. One group will think of reasons why the friendship should not continue. The other group will think of reasons why the friendship should continue.

+ Give each group 5–10 minutes to generate some responses to justify their stance.

+ Choose one child to be the 'victim', ie, the person who shared the secret with the friend they trusted.

+ Divide the groups into two equal sized lines and ask each group to stand facing the other group in a line with a gap or 'alley way' in between.

+ The 'victim' must walk down the alley and move towards individuals standing in the line.

+ If the victim approaches a person standing in the line, that person must give them a reason for either why they should stop being friends with the perpetrator or why they should continue being friends, depending on the group that they have been assigned to.

+ When the victim reaches the end of the 'alley way' they need to make a decision, ie, will they maintain or cease the friendship.

+ Rehearse this drama performance two or three times with the class and then ask them to produce a final performance.

Lesson 4

+ Remind the children that they are learning about breach of trust within friendships.

+ Introduce the strategy of *hot seating*: Ask one child to play the role of victim and explain that they will sit in the hot seat and answer questions from the rest of the class. This needs to be a confident child who can give detailed responses to questions.

+ Ask the rest of the class to think in pairs of a question they can pose to the victim. Ask them to write their questions down on a small whiteboard. Questions might include:

  − What was your secret?
  − Why did you share it with your friend?
  − How did you feel after you shared it with your friend?
  − How did you feel about yourself when you discovered they had not kept your secret?
  − How did you feel about your friend when you discovered they had not kept your secret?
  − How does your friend feel now? How do you know this?
  − Will you be friends with them again? Why do you think this?
  − Will you share a secret with them again? Explain your response.

+ This activity will prepare the children for the next task which is to produce a piece of persuasive writing. Ask them to pretend to be the perpetrator. The friend who shared the secret with them is currently not speaking to them. Their task is to write a letter to their friend to persuade them to forgive them and to offer them reassurance that they will not repeat this mistake in the future. In the letter they should:

  − offer an apology;
  − give reasons for why they broke the trust by telling others about the secret;
  − acknowledge how this made the victim feel;
  − offer reassurances that they will not repeat the mistake.

UNHEALTHY FRIENDSHIPS

The statutory framework (DfE, 2019a) requires children to recognise whether to trust someone within a friendship and to be able to identify when a friendship is making them feel happy, upset or uncomfortable. Children need to know how to seek advice in these situations.

CRITICAL QUESTIONS

+ How might a scheme of work be structured to address the theme of 'caring friendships' across all year groups within a primary school so that learning is well-sequenced and secures progression in knowledge?

+ How might the theme of 'caring friendships' be addressed in the early years?

+ What issues might occur within friendships as children progress from Key Stage 1 to Key Stage 2 and what are the implications for curriculum planning?

SUMMARY

This chapter has emphasised the importance of friendships and it has highlighted the responsibilities placed upon schools in relation to teaching children about friendships. The chapter has also outlined the differences between online and offline relationships and some key considerations have been provided to support your reflection. The characteristics of caring relationships have been identified and practical guidance offered to support your teaching. Case study material has been provided to illuminate effective practice. The chapter has also identified some of the challenges associated with friendships and it has emphasised the importance of children being taught how to recognise unhealthy friendships.

FURTHER READING OR SOURCES OF FURTHER INFORMATION

BBC Bitesize (nd) PSHE and Citizenship: Friendship, Key Stage 1. [online] Available at: www.bbc.co.uk/bitesize/topics/zswwxnb (accessed 30 January 2020).

BBC Bitesize (nd) PSHE and Citizenship: Friendship, Key Stage 2. [online] Available at: www.bbc.co.uk/bitesize/topics/zy77hyc (accessed 30 January 2020).

Kennedy-Moore, E and McLaughlin, C (2017) Growing Friendships: A Kids' Guide to Making and Keeping Friends. London: Aladdin.

Krasny Brown, L and Brown, M (2001) How to be a Friend: A Guide to Making Friends and Keeping Them. New York: Little, Brown Books for Young Readers.

✚ CHAPTER 4

RESPECTFUL RELATIONSHIPS

CHAPTER OBJECTIVES

After reading this chapter you will understand:

+ the need to teach children about mutual respect;

+ the types of bullying and cyberbullying that children must understand;

+ the concepts of harassment, denigration, flaming, impersonation, outing and trickery, cyber-stalking and exclusion;

+ how to support children to understand the role of the internet in relation to intimidation, manipulation and grooming;

+ your role in supporting children to challenge stereotypes.

INTRODUCTION

This chapter emphasises the importance of children being taught to understand mutual respect. It also explains the implications of the statutory guidance in relation to your teaching to support children to develop respectful relationships. The chapter outlines the concept of respect as a fundamental British value and some examples of individuals' differences are outlined to support your understanding. Additionally, the chapter outlines the different types of bullying and cyberbullying children must be able to recognise and some guidance is offered to support your understanding of these. The concepts of harassment, denigration, flaming, impersonation, outing and trickery, cyber-stalking and exclusion are also explained. Finally, the chapter explores the responsibility of schools to educate children in relation to intimidation, manipulation and grooming, and it emphasises the role of schools in supporting children to recognise and challenge stereotyping.

DEVELOPING RESPECTFUL RELATIONSHIPS

Effective relationships are underpinned by mutual respect. The statutory guidance states that children need to know:

+ *the importance of respecting others, including the need to respect people who are different from them. This includes people with different physical appearance, character, personality, background or those who make different choices or have different preferences or beliefs;*

+ *steps they can take to facilitate respectful relationships;*

+ *the conventions of courtesy and manners;*

+ *that respect is mutual;*

+ *the need to respect those in positions of authority;*

+ *the need to gain permission in relationships with friends, peers and adults;*

+ *the importance of giving in relationships.*

(DfE, 2019a, pp 21–2)

Respecting people who are different is one of the fundamental British values. Difference can take many forms including, but not restricted to, physical appearance, personality, social background, cultural diversity, disability, sexual orientation, sex, gender, age and religion or belief. Fundamentally, children need to know that they have a responsibility to respect other people irrespective of any differences. Understanding this principle supports their development as good citizens. It also contributes to the development of an inclusive society. Through Relationships Education, children can begin to understand that our differences make us unique and that differences are something which should be celebrated, not just tolerated.

A well-designed Relationships Education curriculum will teach children the steps that they need to take to support them in developing respectful relationships. These include:

+ the need for negotiation within relationships;

+ the importance of listening to others;

+ the importance of upholding trust;

+ the need to respect confidentiality;

+ the value of demonstrating empathy;

+ the need to seek permission within relationships;

+ the importance of giving: this is not just monetary but also includes giving time and support and showing kindness;

+ the importance of courtesy and good manners.

Children should understand their responsibilities towards others in relationships. They also need to understand the importance of showing respect to people in positions of authority, including teachers. Many children will understand this because they will have been raised to demonstrate respect towards their parents, grandparents and other people in their family. However, some children are not raised in environments where respect towards authority is instilled. These children may start their education not demonstrating respect towards adults who are in positions of authority. They will then encounter resistance from adults, often for the first time. All children need to learn to adjust their behaviour in different contexts (social, cultural, family and educational contexts). However, children who have not been raised in environments where respect for authority is insisted upon and modelled by adults may take longer to adjust to the expectations within the school. These children may benefit from an intervention which is specifically designed to develop their social and emotional regulation skills.

CRITICAL QUESTIONS

+ Why is respect important within relationships?
+ What are the warning signs which might suggest that a relationship is not based on mutual respect?

THE IMPORTANCE OF SELF RESPECT

The statutory framework states that children need to know the importance of self respect and how this links to their own happiness (DfE, 2019a). If you have self respect, you hold the belief that you are a good person and therefore deserve to be treated well. For example, if you believe that you should be treated well, you will not tolerate other people lying to you or treating you unfairly. People with low self esteem may demonstrate low self respect or have no self respect. Self respect is important for personal happiness. Children who have experienced abuse or neglect may have low self respect.

Self respect can be taught through Relationships Education. The experience of success in school can develop children's self esteem and this will support them to feel good about themselves. However, children also need to know that everyone has weaknesses and imperfections, everyone makes mistakes and everyone has the capacity to grow and change. Regardless of their imperfections and weaknesses children should be taught that they are worthy individuals who deserve respect and they should expect this from others. Children also need to understand that although it feels good to get approval from others, fundamentally they should feel good about themselves and are entitled to be treated with respect because they are human.

BULLYING

The statutory framework states that children need to know about different types of bullying which can occur within relationships, including cyberbullying, the responsibilities of bystanders to report the bullying and how to get help (DfE, 2019a). Children need to be taught to recognise bullying within relationships by understanding that physical bullying is only one type of bullying. They need to be able to recognise that bullying may also include:

+ emotional bullying in which perpetrators seek to undermine a person's self worth and self respect;

+ acts of manipulation;

+ acts of micro-aggression which could include ignoring someone, moving away from someone or other forms of non-verbal bullying;

+ cyberbullying.

Bullying may be homophobic, racist, religious, sizeist, disablist or sexist. People's differences in physical appearance, personality and belief can be the motivator for bullying and therefore the curriculum should cover each of these different aspects.

CYBERBULLYING

Cyberbullying is bullying that takes place over the internet, including bullying which takes place on social media. It takes a variety of forms. These include:

+ *posting hurtful comments;*

+ *posting videos which are targeted directly at a person to cause distress;*

+ *posting photographs which are designed to cause distress;*

+ *inciting others to make hurtful comments aimed at a person;*

+ *sending hurtful text messages using a mobile phone;*

+ *sending hurtful private messages to a person.*

(Glazzard and Mitchell, 2018)

Types of cyberbullying are addressed below, taken from Glazzard and Mitchell (2018).

HARASSMENT

Harassment is the act of sending offensive, rude and insulting messages and being abusive. It includes nasty or humiliating comments on posts, on photos and in chat rooms and making offensive comments on gaming sites. Posting false and malicious things about people on the internet can be classed as harassment.

DENIGRATION

This is when someone may send information about another person that is fake, damaging and untrue. It includes sharing photographs of someone for the purpose of ridiculing and spreading fake rumours and gossip. This can be on any site online or on apps. It includes purposely altering photographs of others to ridicule and cause distress.

FLAMING

Flaming is when someone purposely uses extreme and offensive language and deliberately gets into online arguments and fights. They do this to deliberately cause distress in others.

IMPERSONATION

Impersonation is when someone hacks into someone's email or social networking account and uses the person's online identity to send or post vicious or embarrassing material to or about others. It also includes making up fake profiles of others.

OUTING AND TRICKERY

This is when someone shares personal information about someone else or tricks someone into revealing secrets and subsequently forwards it to others. This may also involve the sharing or distribution of private or personal images and videos.

CYBER-STALKING

Cyber-stalking is the act of repeatedly sending messages that include threats of harm, harassment, intimidating messages, or engaging in other online activities that make a person afraid for their safety. The actions may be illegal depending on what they are doing. Cyber-stalking can take place on the internet or via mobile phones. Examples include:

+ silent calls;

+ insulting and threatening texts;

+ abusive verbal messages;

+ cases of stolen identity.

EXCLUSION

This is when others intentionally leave someone out of a group such as group messages, online apps, gaming sites and other online engagement. This is also a form of social bullying and is very common.

BULLYING BY SPREADING RUMOURS AND GOSSIP

Online abuse, rumours and gossip can go viral very quickly and be shared by many people within several minutes. It is not uncommon for former close friends or partners to share personal secrets about victims.

THREATENING BEHAVIOUR

Threatening behaviour that is directed at a victim to cause alarm and distress is a criminal offence. Taking screenshots of the evidence and reporting it is one way of challenging this.

HAPPY SLAPPING

This is an incident where a person is assaulted while other people take photographs or videos on their mobile phones. The pictures or videos are then circulated by mobile phone or uploaded on the internet.

GROOMING

Grooming is when someone builds an emotional connection with a child to gain their trust for the purposes of abuse and exploitation. It is conducted by strangers (or new 'friends') and may include:

+ pressurising someone to do something they do not wish to do;

+ making someone take their clothes off;

+ pressurising someone to engage in sexual conversations;

+ pressurising someone to take naked photographs of themselves;

+ making someone engage in sexual activity via the internet.

Groomers may spend a long time establishing a 'relationship' with the victim by using the following strategies:

+ *pretending to be someone they are not, for example saying they are the same age online;*

+ *offering advice or understanding;*

+ *buying gifts;*

+ *giving the child attention;*

+ *using their professional position or reputation;*

+ *giving compliments;*

+ *taking them on trips, outings or holidays.*

(www.nspcc.org.uk, accessed 30 January 2020)

It is against the law for anyone under the age of 18 to take, send or redistribute indecent pictures of anyone under the age of 18. Groomers can be male or female and they can be of any age.

CEOP is the Child Exploitation and Online Protection Command which investigates cases of sexual abuse and grooming on the internet.

INAPPROPRIATE IMAGES

It is very easy to save any pictures of anyone on any site and upload them to the internet. Uploading pictures of someone to cause distress is a form of cyberbullying. This also includes digitally altering pictures to embarrass someone.

BYSTANDER EFFECT

Witnessing cyberbullying and doing nothing about it is not acceptable. Some people are worried about getting involved but victims of bullying need brave witnesses to make a stand. Perpetrators of bullying thrive when they have an audience. Making a stand against what they are doing is one way of reducing their power. Most sites now operate a reporting facility so that online abuse can be reported and addressed. Bystanders are not innocent. They have a responsibility to report abuse that they witness.

CASE STUDY

BULLYING

YEAR 3, PSHE

This unit of work will cover different types of bullying, including homo-phobic bullying, disablist bullying, racism or bullying due to social back-ground. The content will be distributed over four lessons and this case study addresses the first lesson.

Lesson 1

+ Ask the children if they have heard the word 'gay' being used in a bad way. Provide them with an opportunity to give feedback.

+ Ask the children to explain their understanding of the word 'gay'.

+ Explain the meaning of the word 'gay'.

+ Explain that the word is often used inappropriately, for example 'that pencil case is so gay'. Ask the children what the word 'gay' means in the context of this sentence (that pencil case is so gay = that pencil case is so rubbish).

+ Explain that when 'gay' is used to represent 'rubbish' this is not acceptable. Ask the children how this might make someone feel.

+ Can they think of other examples of when 'gay' is used inappropriately?

+ Ask them to work in groups. Move them to tables and provide them with a selection of cards and two sorting hoops. One sorting hoop denotes a correct use of the word 'gay' and the other sorting hoop denotes a bad use of the word 'gay'.

+ Provide the children with a variety of statements and ask them to sort each statement into the correct sorting hoop (for example, 'That toy is gay'; 'Someone in my family is gay').

+ Invite the children to provide feedback on the activity and model the correct responses on the board.

STEREOTYPES

The statutory framework states that children need to know what a stereotype is and understand how stereotypes can be unfair, negative or destructive (DfE, 2019a). Children can develop stereotypes about a variety of things but gender stereotypes are particularly common. Children are socialised into gender roles from birth which result in them developing very specific ideas about what it means to be a boy and what it means to be a girl. Stereotypes are reinforced by parents through the clothes that children wear, the toys they are given to play with, the hobbies and interests they are encouraged and supported to pursue, and the clear messages that parents transmit to children in relation to what it means to be a boy or a girl. These stereotypes are also reinforced through the media, through the stories that children read and by peers who regulate the boundaries of acceptable behaviour. The well-known and much loved story of *The Tiger Who Came to Tea* by Judith Kerr reinforced many gender stereotypes in that it highlighted clear differences in gender roles between the main characters.

The problem with gender stereotyping is that it limits opportunities. Girls grow up thinking that they cannot participate in hobbies, subjects and job roles that are traditionally associated with males. The reverse is also true. Gender stereotyping is evident in all aspects of life. Clothes, cars, other possessions, activities and colours are often associated with a specific gender. It leads to the development of unhealthy assumptions. One example of this is the assumption that boys should be strong and powerful and not show their emotions. This can result in some males developing very serious mental health problems because they may believe that it is wrong to express their emotions. This demonstrates how dangerous and incorrect gender stereotyping can be.

This artificial division between genders is problematic because it is based on the assumption that gender is a binary, and this is not the case. Additionally, children who demonstrate characteristics which do not align with the expected gender norms are at risk of experiencing homophobic bullying. The Relationships Education curriculum should support children to think critically about the stereotypes and the assumptions that underpin them. It should support children to challenge the stereotypes and introduce them to role models. Examples may include females or males from the local community who do jobs that are not typically associated with their gender, for example scientists, engineers or professional footballers who are women.

Stereotypes exist not only in relation to gender, but also in relation to, but not limited to, race, religion, disability, social or cultural background and age.

CRITICAL QUESTIONS

+ What stereotypes exist in relation to the characteristics identified above?

+ Why is it important to challenge stereotypes?

CASE STUDY

CHALLENGING STEREOTYPES

YEAR 2, PSHE/ENGLISH

The following lessons are part of a unit of work on challenging stereotypes. The unit aims to develop the children's knowledge of stereotypes and understand why stereotypes are wrong.

Lesson 1

+ Read the story of *Morris Micklewhite and the Tangerine Dress* by Christine Baldacchino. The main character, Morris, loves his tangerine dress. He is bullied by his peers because of the dress but eventually they decide that this does not matter.

+ Ask the children to retell the story.

+ Ask them to imagine how Morris must have felt when he was ridiculed by his peers for wearing the dress. Present the class with a large sheet of paper with an outline of Morris. Using marker pens, ask them to write down words to describe how Morris might have felt when he was teased.

+ Explain to the children that we grow up believing that boys and girls should wear different clothes. Ask them to provide examples.

+ Explain that there is no such thing as 'girls' or 'boys' clothes and that children can wear any clothes that they choose to wear.

+ Show the children images of men and women wearing clothes that do not conform to the gender stereotypes, for example outside Western cultures, men's clothing commonly includes skirts and skirt-like garments, and explain that skirts have been worn since prehistoric times. They were the standard dressing for men and women in all ancient cultures.

Lesson 2

+ Read *The Tiger Who Came to Tea* by Judith Kerr.

+ Ask the children to work in groups to order illustrations from the story in the correct order to show the sequence of events in the story.

+ Discuss the roles of Mum and Dad in the story.

+ Explain that these roles are very traditional because the story is a very old story.

+ Explain that in many families today, both parents go out to work and both parents share the responsibility of raising children and cooking meals.

+ Ask the children to talk in pairs about the roles of the different people within their families.

+ Ask the children to rewrite the story in sequence using time-related vocabulary, for example, *first, next, then, after that, finally.*

Lesson 3

+ Invite someone into class from the community who has a job which does not align with traditional gender roles, for example, a male carer.

+ Ask them to talk to the children about the different aspects of their job role.

+ Ask the children to think of a question to ask the visitor. Give them thinking time in pairs to generate a question.

+ Provide the children with an opportunity to ask their questions.

+ Record the questions and responses from the speaker so that you can create a display.

+ Ask the children to write a non-chronological report on the role of a carer (the features of non-chronological reports must have been taught previously).

Lesson 4

+ Show the children photographs of selected famous people who have job roles which challenge gender stereotypes.

+ Teach the elements of story structure.

+ Ask them to write a story about a character who is not a typical boy or typical girl.

+ Provide them with a story board to plan the story.

+ Ask them to plan the story using the story board. They will need to plan a setting for the story. They will need to plan the key events in the story, the main problem (climax), resolution and ending.

+ Ask them to complete the story board.

Lesson 5

+ The children will continue planning their story on the story board.

+ Ask them to orally rehearse the story with their talk partner.

+ Their talk partner will provide them with feedback on their story and they will use this feedback to amend their story board.

+ Ask them to use their story board to start writing the story.

Lesson 6

+ In this lesson the children will continue writing their stories.

+ They will self assess their stories against specified success criteria.

SUMMARY

This chapter has emphasised the importance of children being taught to understand mutual respect. It has also explained the implications of the statutory guidance in relation to your teaching. Case study material has been provided to illuminate effective practice and a range of questions have been asked to support your reflection. The chapter has also outlined the concept of respect as a fundamental British value and it has provided some examples of individuals' differences to support your teaching. Additionally, the chapter has outlined the different types of bullying and cyberbullying that children must be able to recognise. Guidance has been offered to support your understanding of these. The chapter has outlined the concepts of harassment, denigration, flaming, impersonation, outing and trickery, cyber-stalking and exclusion and it has emphasised the role of schools in supporting children to understand these. Finally, the chapter has explored the responsibility of schools to educate children in relation to intimidation, manipulation and grooming and it has emphasised the importance of children being able to recognise and challenge stereotyping.

FURTHER READING OR SOURCES OF FURTHER INFORMATION

Broadbent, T (2017) *Switched on Online Safety Key Stage 2*. Oxon: Rising Stars.

Equality and Human Rights Commission (2016) Learning Area 2: Challenging Stereotypes and Discrimination. [online] Available at: www.equalityhumanrights.com/en/primary-education-resources/lesson-activity-ideas/learning-area-2-challenging-stereotypes-and (accessed 8 November 2019).

Sanders, J and Jennings, S (2017) *Let's Talk About Body Boundaries, Consent and Respect*. Victoria, AU: Educate2Empower Publishing.

Teach Primary (2011) PSHE Lesson Plan: Challenging Stereotypes. [online] Available at: www.teachprimary.com/learning_resources/view/pshe-lesson-plan-challenging-stereotypes (assessed 8 November 2019).

✚ CHAPTER 5
BEING SAFE

CHAPTER OBJECTIVES

After reading this chapter you will understand:

✚ your role in relation to supporting children to recognise and establish boundaries in relationships;

✚ the requirement of schools to teach children to stay safe online;

✚ the importance of children understanding how to report concerns and receive support with these;

✚ the requirements of the statutory guidance in relation to secrecy and disclosure.

INTRODUCTION

This chapter outlines the responsibility of schools in relation to supporting children to understand appropriate boundaries in relationships. It provides examples of these boundaries to support your teaching and it offers some critical questions to encourage you to reflect on your current understanding. The chapter also offers guidance which you may wish to consider when you are planning and delivering activities relating to online safety. Additionally, it outlines some examples of how children can report concerns and seek support and we emphasise the importance of children being taught this information. Finally, the chapter discusses disclosure and secrecy in the context of the statutory guidance and case study material is provided to illuminate effective practice.

ESTABLISHING BOUNDARIES IN RELATIONSHIPS

Through Relationships Education children need to understand that they have a right to create boundaries within the relationships that they establish. Individuals retain the right to set healthy boundaries in relation to:

+ physical contact that is permitted;

+ respect for personal body space;

+ how they expect others to treat them within relationships;

+ the values and beliefs that will be accepted within relationships;

+ the amount of time that they are prepared to invest in the relationship;

+ how contact will be maintained throughout the relationship;

+ character traits which will not be permitted;

+ character traits which will be valued within the relationship.

CRITICAL QUESTIONS

+ What boundaries are important to you within relationships?

+ How might these boundaries change within different relationships?

53

STAYING SAFE ONLINE

The statutory guidance states that children need to understand that people may behave differently online, including by pretending to be someone they are not. They need to understand the importance of respecting other people online and the rules and principles for keeping safe online. Children need to be able to recognise the risks associated with being online, recognise harmful content and contact and know how to report them. The following guidelines will support children in staying safe online.

+ *Don't post any personal information online, including your address, email address or mobile number.*

+ *Think carefully before posting pictures or videos of yourself. Once you've put a picture of yourself online most people can see it and may be able to download it, it's not just yours anymore.*

+ *Keep your privacy settings as high as possible.*

+ *Never give out your passwords.*

+ *Don't befriend people you don't know.*

+ *Don't meet up with people you've met online. Speak to your parent or carer about people suggesting you do.*

+ *Remember that not everyone online is who they say they are.*

+ *Think carefully about what you say before you post something online.*

+ *Respect other people's views, even if you don't agree with someone else's views doesn't mean you need to be rude.*

+ *If you see something online that makes you feel uncomfortable, unsafe or worried: leave the website, turn off your computer if you want to and tell a trusted adult immediately.*

(www.safetynetkids.org.uk/personal-safety/staying-safe-online/, accessed 30 January 2020)

The concept of digital citizenship is a useful one for children to be introduced to. They need to know what the attributes of a good digital citizen are. These can be contrasted with the attributes of a bad digital citizen. Fundamentally, children need to understand that the concept of citizenship applies in both the offline and online worlds. They need to know that people deserve to be treated with respect regardless of the fact that interactions are conducted online and sometimes anonymously. Children therefore need to understand their responsibilities as digital citizens. Children need appropriate digital literacy skills to be able to protect themselves online. For example, they need to know how to block or mute people, how to protect their accounts and how to report abuse.

CRITICAL QUESTIONS

+ What are the attributes of a good digital citizen?

+ How can children be supported, through Relationships Education, to critically analyse digital content?

HOW TO GET HELP

Through Relationships Education, children begin to understand the importance of reporting online behaviour which makes them feel uncomfortable, sad or distressed. They need to understand the importance of talking to someone who they can trust. This may be a teacher, peer or someone in the family or their community. Children need to know that information that they have shared cannot always be kept confidential. People who they have disclosed the information to may need to pass the information on to someone else to keep them safe. However, regardless, they have a right to know what information has been shared, who it has been shared with and what will happen next. Children should also be introduced to important organisations, including Childline, the Child Exploitation and Online Protection Command (CEOP) and the National Society for the Prevention of Cruelty to Children (NSPCC).

+ Childline offers free and confidential advice and support to under 18 year-olds who do not feel safe.

+ Children can make a report to CEOP if they are worried about someone making them feel uncomfortable online.

+ The NSPCC runs a 24-hour child protection helpline for adults who are worried about a child's safety.

CRITICAL QUESTIONS

+ Why might some children be reluctant to tell others when they are being exploited or abused online?

+ How can children be supported, through Relationships Education, to challenge online abuse that they have witnessed (bystander effect)?

+ When should children ask for help?

CASE STUDY

PHYSICAL CONTACT

YEAR 1, PSHE/SCIENCE

This series of lessons supports children to understand the rules about physical contact.

Lesson 1

+ Inform the children that this lesson will enable them to learn about safe and unsafe touch.

+ Invite the children to consider why people might touch other people. What do they think 'safe touch' means? What is 'unsafe touch'?

+ Examples of unsafe touches might include hitting, punching, kicking or touching one's private parts.

+ Ask the children to work in pairs.

+ Provide each pair with a set of cards with images on and captions to depict safe and unsafe touch.

+ Ask the children to look at the cards and to sort them into the two categories.

Lesson 2

+ Explain that in this lesson they will learn about how our relationship with other people affects the rules about touching.

+ Show the children pictures which depict close physical contact. Examples include hugging and kissing. Ask them to think about which people in their lives they would allow to demonstrate this type of contact. Examples might include parents or grandparents.

+ Show the children pictures which depict less close physical contact. Examples include handshakes. Ask them to think about which people in their lives they would allow to demonstrate this type of contact. Examples might include friends.

+ Show the children pictures which depict no physical contact. Examples include waving or showing a thumbs-up. Ask them to think about which people in their lives should not usually need to demonstrate physical contact towards them. Examples might include teachers. Are there any times when the rules on physical contact might need to change?

+ Ask the children to work in groups. Provide them with cards which show different categories of people. Examples include brother, sister, cousin, parent, grandparent, friend and teacher. This range can be extended to include people within the community or people from the extended family. Ask them to sort the cards into three categories as follows:

 − close contact;
 − some contact;
 − no contact.

+ Ask the children to consider whether someone who usually has no physical contact is allowed to demonstrate physical contact, for example, a teacher might need to use physical contact if a child has become hurt. Ask them to consider whether specific people could fall into more than one of the three groups.

Lesson 3

+ Explain to the children that in this lesson they will learn about who is allowed to touch their private parts.

+ Ask the children to think about parts of the body that should not be touched. Display an image of a body with the body parts labelled. Ask the children to identify which parts can be touched and which parts should not be touched. Ensure that children know the correct name for external body parts, including the reproductive organs and other private parts of the body.

+ Challenge the children to think about which people may be allowed to touch their private parts. Examples include doctors or nurses. Ask them to think of reasons why these people may need to touch them.

+ Explain to the children that parents may sometimes need to touch their child's private parts. This is appropriate if they need to clean them or check for damage but usually they should not touch them.

+ Explain to the children that people should not touch their bodies without their permission. They are in charge of their own body.

+ Give the children an outline of the human body and ask them to label the external body parts. Once they have labelled the body parts ask them to cross out using a red coloured pencil the labels of the body parts that other people should never touch.

Lesson 4

+ Explain that in this lesson the children will learn about personal space.

+ Ask them to tell you what they understand by 'personal space'.

+ Demonstrate the concept of personal space by asking for two volunteers.

+ Ask them to stand up and move very close to each other so that personal space is invaded.

+ Ask them to describe how this made them feel.

+ Explain to the children that everyone has personal space which some people do not like other people to move into. Some people don't mind this but other people do mind if their personal space is invaded. Also explain that acceptable distances vary between individuals.

+ Ask the children to get into pairs.

+ Ask them to stand four strides away from each other but facing each other. Ask them to describe how this makes them feel.

+ Then ask one person to move one stride closer to their partner. The partner stands still. Ask them both to say how they feel now.

+ Repeat by asking one person to gradually move forward towards the other person. Find the point when both people are so close that they start to feel uncomfortable.

+ Then ask them to swap over so that both children have an opportunity to be the person who stands still and the person who moves forward.

+ Ask them to find a different partner and to repeat the activity.

+ Ask the children to think about which people they might sometimes allow to invade their personal space. Then ask them to think about who is never allowed to invade their personal space.

SECRETS

The statutory guidance states that children need to be taught that it is not always right to keep a secret because sometimes this does not keep them safe. The sequence of lessons which follows supports children to distinguish between when it is right to keep a secret and when it is not right.

CASE STUDY

SECRETS

YEAR 3, PSHE/ENGLISH

In this unit of work the children will learn about secrets. They will learn what a secret is, when it is right to keep a secret and when it is right to share the secret with others.

Lesson 1

+ The objective of this lesson is for the children to learn about what secrets are.

+ Ask the children if they have ever had a secret that no one knows.

+ Ask them to think about the types of secrets that people might keep.

+ Explain to the children that some secrets can be kept secret but some should never be kept. Give them an example:

  – *A friend tells you that you must give them money each week and that you must keep this a secret. This is a secret which must be shared.*
  – *A friend tells you that they are frightened of dogs. This secret does not need to be shared.*

+ In the first example ask the children to think about why the friend wants you to keep the secret.

+ Ask them to think about why the second secret does not need to be shared.

+ Provide them with some scenarios similar to the two examples and ask them to decide if the secret needs to be kept or if it needs to be shared. This is a paired task so that the children get an opportunity to discuss the scenarios.

+ As a class generate some general principles for when a secret should be kept and when a secret should be shared. Make two lists to reflect this.

+ Ask them to privately think about if they have ever kept a secret which they should have shared with someone. Inform them that they can talk to someone they trust about this but remind them that the information may need to be shared with others if they are in danger so that they can be kept safe. Explain to the children that if someone shares a secret with them and they consider that person to be in danger then the secret must be passed on to a teacher.

Lesson 2

+ The objective of this lesson is for the children to learn about secrets that must be shared.

+ Introduce the children to the following scenario. Harley is being bullied by Freddie. Freddie makes Harley hand over his sweets. Freddie threatens to hurt Harley if Harley refuses to do what Freddie wants him to do. He tells Harley that he must keep this a secret or face consequences. This carries on for a few weeks. Then Freddie asks Harley to hand over any money he has. Harley is anxious about going to school but is too frightened to report it.

+ Ask the children to imagine how Harley feels. What is Freddie doing to Harley? Why is Harley frightened? Why does Freddie ask Harley to keep it a secret? What might happen if Harley doesn't tell anyone what is happening?

+ Explain to the children about the importance of sharing secrets like this. Tell the children that they are going to write a persuasive letter to Harley to convince him to share the secret with someone that they trust. In the letter they need to provide reasons to convince Harley to share the secret.

+ The features of persuasive writing will already have been taught in English but the children will need to be reminded of them.

+ Using live modelling, model the first few sentences of the letter. Then ask the children to write their own letters. Some children may need a writing frame or sentence openers to scaffold the writing process.

Lesson 3

+ The objective of this lesson is for the children to learn when to keep a secret and when to disclose a secret.

+ Ask the children to think about if they have ever kept a secret. When might it be important to keep a secret? When is it important to disclose a secret?

+ In this lesson they will work in pairs to write secrets that should be kept and secrets that should be shared.

+ The teacher will model how to write a secret on a slip of paper.

+ Provide the children with secret slips. Ask them to work in pairs to write secrets on the slips (one secret per slip). Ask them to write down secrets which should be kept secret as well as secrets which should be shared.

+ Ask each pair to read their secrets and to sort them into two piles, ie, secrets to keep and secrets to share.

+ Explain to the class that secrets which make people feel unsafe should always be shared.

Lesson 4

+ The objective of this lesson is for the children to learn about risky behaviour.

+ Introduce the children to the following scenario: Oscar is in Year 3. His mother and father have divorced and his mother has met a new partner (Jack) who he gets to know well. Oscar likes Jack and he enjoys spending time with him. One evening Oscar's mum goes out to meet her friends and leaves Jack in charge of Oscar. Oscar and Jack start chatting and then decide to watch a film. After a while Oscar becomes tired and falls asleep next to Jack on the sofa. When Oscar wakes up an hour later he finds that Jack is stroking his hair. Oscar feels uncomfortable but Jack tells him that he has lovely hair and that this is their secret.

+ Ask the class what they think Oscar should do. Is this safe behaviour or unsafe behaviour? Ask them to justify their responses.

+ Ask them to imagine that Oscar is their friend. Put the children into pairs and ask them to do some paired improvisation. One person in the pair should pretend to be Oscar and the other person should be Oscar's friend. Imagine that Oscar is about to share the secret. Think through what Oscar will say and how the friend might respond.

+ Give the children time to practise their improvisations.

+ Ask some of the pairs to perform their improvisations.

+ Explain to the children that this is not safe behaviour because Jack has touched Oscar without permission. Emphasise the importance of seeking permission for bodily contact within friendships and other relationships.

Lesson 5

+ The objective of this lesson is for the children to learn about online risks.

+ Introduce the children to the following scenario: George and Austin are communicating online via a messaging service. Austin and George are in the same class. Austin starts being mean to George on the messaging platform but he is nice with him in person. Austin tells George to keep the nasty messages a secret otherwise he will be nasty to George in school. On the messaging platform Austin makes offensive comments about George's hair colour and his size. These comments are distressing for George. George does not tell anyone but the messages over time become increasingly hurtful.

+ Ask the class how they think George should respond. Discuss the importance of talking to someone that George can trust and also the options that George has to block Austin on the messaging platform and to take a screenshot of the conversation as evidence.

+ Explain to the children the range of options that George has available to him to help him to stay safe. He can talk to his parents, another friend or a teacher. He can report the abuse to the messaging platform or he can take a screenshot.

+ The lesson is a writing lesson.

+ The children will write a dialogue between two people using a messaging platform in which the conversation illustrates that one person is being bullied. The teacher will need to model this first. In the dialogue, the victim should provide the perpetrator with an opportunity to stop what they are doing by explaining what steps that they will take if the bullying does not stop.

SUMMARY

This chapter has outlined the responsibility of schools in relation to supporting children to understand appropriate boundaries in relationships. It has provided examples of these boundaries to support your teaching and it has offered some critical questions to encourage you to reflect on your current understanding. The chapter has also offered guidance which you may wish to consider when you are planning and delivering activities relating to online safety. Additionally, it has outlined some examples of how children can report concerns and seek support and we have emphasised the importance of children being taught this information. Finally, the chapter has discussed disclosure and secrecy in the context of the statutory guidance and case study material has been provided to illuminate effective practice.

FURTHER READING OR SOURCES OF FURTHER INFORMATION

Videos on staying safe online

Online Safety: Staying Safe Online. Discovery Education UK. Available at: www.youtube.com/watch?v=aMSHtE42mmI (accessed 4 February 2020).

Being Safe on the Internet. AMAZE Org. Available at: www.youtube.com/watch?v=HxySrSbSY7o (accessed 4 February 2020).

5 Internet Safety Tips for Kids. Common Sense Media. Available at: www.youtube.com/watch?v=X9Htg8V3eik (accessed 4 February 2020).

EYFS resources

Digiduck's Big Decision. Available at: www.childnet.com/resources/digiducks-big-decision (accessed 4 February 2020).

The Adventures of Smartie the Penguin E-book. Available at: www.childnet.com/resources/smartie-the-penguin-e-book (accessed 4 February 2020).

Key Stage 1 resources

Beware of Lurking Trolls. Portsmouth City Council. Available at: www.youtube.com/watch?v=d8D8i0fO3Uo (accessed 4 February 2020).

PANTS: The Underwear Rule. Available at: www.nspcc.org.uk/keeping-children-safe/support-for-parents/underwear-rule/?utm_source=google&utm_medium=cpc&utm_campaign=Underwear_Rule_BND_B&utm_term=the_underwear_rule_nspcc&gclid=CIDfqbrzjcACFYofwwodzEwAyQ&gclsrc=aw.ds (accessed 4 February 2020).

Key Stage 2 resources

Staying Safe Online Resources for Key Stage 2. Available at: www.tes.co.uk/teaching-resource/Staying-SafeOnline-Resources-for-Key-Stage-2-6400807/ (accessed 4 February 2020).

Sexting and Sending Nudes. Available at: www.childline.org.uk/info-advice/bullying-abuse-safety/online-mobile-safety/sexting/?utm_source=google&utm_medium=cpc&utm_campaign=NSPCC_-_Sexting&utm_term=facts_about_sexting&gclid=CJefrN2MjsACFQsKwwodXTMAOA&gclsrc=aw.ds (accessed 4 February 2020).

RealLoveRocks. Available at: www.barnardosrealloverocks.org.uk/ (accessed 4 February 2020).

Books

Sherman, J (2006) *Because It's My Body!* SAFE for Children Publishing.

✚CHAPTER 6

PHYSICAL AND MENTAL WELL-BEING

CHAPTER OBJECTIVES

After reading this chapter you will understand:

✚ the importance of children recognising the relationship between physical health and good mental well-being;

✚ the need to support children to manage their online activities;

✚ the role of the curriculum in supporting children to understand the dangers associated with smoking, alcohol use and drug taking;

✚ school responsibilities in relation to teaching children about basic first aid;

✚ the importance of supporting children to recognise the physical and emotional challenges associated with adolescence.

INTRODUCTION

This chapter introduces the requirements of the statutory framework in relation to physical health and good mental well-being. It explains the relationship between these but also emphasises the importance of children being able to recognise and understand how they are different. It also outlines the features of an effective curriculum in relation to physical health and mental well-being and some guidance is offered to support your teaching and planning. Additionally, the chapter highlights the responsibility of schools to teach children about the benefits and risks associated with internet use. The importance of children understanding how to demonstrate good citizenship is then explained within the context of both their online and offline activities. Some guidance is offered to illuminate effective practice and to support you in promoting children's physical health. There is some consideration in relation to the curriculum and how it can support children to understand the dangers associated with smoking, alcohol use and drug taking. Finally, we highlight the role of schools in teaching children about basic first aid and the physical and emotional challenges associated with adolescence.

CURRICULUM OVERVIEW

The statutory framework (DfE, 2019a) emphasises the importance of children understanding the relationship between physical health and good mental well-being. Good physical health contributes to good mental well-being and the curriculum aims to provide children with the know-ledge that they need to stay healthy. Children need to understand the benefits and importance of daily exercise, good nutrition and sufficient sleep. They need to know how to protect their health and well-being and the importance of personal hygiene, a healthy lifestyle, self regulation and self care. The curriculum aims to reduce the stigma associated with mental well-being and it aims to ensure that children understand the importance of social connection and participation in communities, hobbies and interests to maintain good mental well-being.

MENTAL WELL-BEING

The statutory framework aims to educate children about the import-ance of taking care of their mental health. Children need to understand the difference between physical health and mental health but also the relationship between the two. Participation in physical activity improves mental well-being. However, children also need to understand the contribution that a healthy diet, sufficient sleep and social connections can make to their mental health.

The curriculum needs to be age appropriate. Typically, it will begin with children in the early years and Key Stage 1 learning about the normal range of emotions that they will experience. An effective curriculum develops children's emotional literacy by providing them with the language to describe their emotions and strategies to regulate their emotions. In addition, children need to be able to recognise different emotions in their peers and know how to support them; for example, when their friends feel sad, angry or nervous. Developing the skill of emotional regulation is critical to good mental health and children need to develop a range of strategies to support them in this respect. These might include:

+ participating in physical activity;

+ talking to other people about how they feel;

+ taking themselves into a quiet space so that they can reflect;

+ focusing on their breathing when they feel angry;

+ counting to ten before responding when they feel angry;

+ participating in an activity which requires focus and concentration to take their mind off the situation that is causing upset.

CRITICAL QUESTIONS

+ What other strategies can support children to develop the skill of emotional regulation?

+ What factors might result in children experiencing negative emotions?

Teachers need to support children to understand that everyone experiences a range of emotions and that this is a normal part of life. However, it is important that children can recognise when their emotions change and can regulate their emotions so that they do not respond to these in ways that are inappropriate.

As children progress through primary school they will learn about simple self-care techniques, isolation and loneliness, and the impact of bullying (including cyberbullying) on people's mental well-being. It is important that children learn to recognise the triggers which influence their emotions and know how to seek help if they are worried about their own well-being or the well-being of someone else. As children progress into Key Stage 2 they will need to understand different types of mental ill health, including anxiety, depression and self-harm. The curriculum content needs to be age appropriate and accessible. One way of making it accessible is to use story books which include characters that display a range of emotions.

CASE STUDY

MENTAL WELL-BEING

YEAR 5, PSHE

A primary school designed a curriculum for mental health in partnership with a mental health charity. The curriculum covered a range of themes. These included:

+ what is mental health?

+ physical activity and mental health;

+ social connections and mental health;

+ bullying and mental health;

+ loneliness;

+ anxiety;

+ depression;

+ self-harm;

+ social media and gaming;

+ developing resilience;

+ managing stress.

The curriculum was delivered during the autumn term. Some lessons were delivered by the teacher, a representative from the charity delivered some of the lessons and links were also established with the local football club. Local footballers from the club came into school to deliver the lesson on depression. They talked openly with the children about their own experiences of depression, the pressures associated with needing to perform at a high level and the importance of resilience. They also talked to the children about the relationship between physical and mental well-being. This lesson helped the children to reframe the stereotype that some of them held about males and mental health in that some of them thought that men should not cry or feel upset.

During the session on loneliness the charity brokered the support of two university students who came into school to talk about their experiences of loneliness. They addressed the factors that had resulted in them experiencing loneliness and they explained the steps they had taken to overcome loneliness. This helped the children to reframe their stereotypes in that they had previously associated loneliness with older people.

The charity put the school in contact with a young man who had been a gaming addict but had overcome the problem. He frequently visited primary and secondary schools to talk about his experiences of gaming, including the devastating effects that gaming had on his life.

The children enjoyed the curriculum because they valued the opportunity to hear so many voices. The school also developed a partnership with a community organisation that supported elderly people to participate in a day centre. The elderly people visited the centre to meet other people and to participate in a range of activities. The purpose was to bring people together to break the cycle of loneliness. The school approached the centre to ask if the children could volunteer by talking to the elderly people. The Year 5 class visited the centre one afternoon a week for half a term. To add structure to the visit, the programme was designed to support a local history unit that the children were studying. The children planned questions and interviewed the elderly people about what life was like in the past. The children then brought the information back to school and this was used to support work in history, English and geography. Sometimes the children played games with the elderly people. The programme facilitated links between the school and the community and enabled children to become active members of their community, thus promoting a civic mindset.

INTERNET SAFETY AND RISKS

A well-designed digital curriculum will teach children about the benefits of the internet but also the importance of rationing the time they spend online. Children need to understand the risks associated with excessive screen time and the impact of this on their own health and the health of other people around them. Children need to understand the importance of demonstrating good citizenship, both online and offline. In addition, they need to understand the benefits and risks associated with social media, including the benefits and risks associated with online gaming. Children need to be aware of a range of risks, including online abuse, bullying, trolling and grooming. They need to develop digital literacy skills so that they can keep themselves safe online and they need to know how to access support if they experience negative online content or interactions.

PHYSICAL HEALTH

Children need to understand the association between physical health and mental well-being and the benefits associated with regular exercise. Many primary schools now require children to complete the 'daily mile'. This is where children complete one mile of vigorous physical activity per day. Children need to know the risks associated with inactivity, including health conditions such as obesity. The curriculum should also teach children about the importance of eating healthily and how to look after their teeth. As children progress through school they need to understand the role of alcohol in adulthood and the impact of alcohol on health.

The curriculum should introduce children to the importance of good dental health and oral hygiene. It should highlight the importance of self care including the need for good quality sleep, personal hygiene, immunisation and vaccination. It should also introduce children to the risks associated with over-exposure to the sun, including skin cancer.

CASE STUDY

PHYSICAL HEALTH

PRIMARY, CROSS-CURRICULAR

A cluster of primary schools across the north-west of England developed a partnership with a local university. The university developed a wristband challenge. By completing weekly physical activity children would work towards a bronze, silver or gold wristband. The physical activity could be completed during school time or after school. The children were required to keep a record of the physical activity that they had participated in by completing a record sheet and this had to be signed each week by either a parent or teacher.

Children first worked towards achieving the bronze wristband. By completing increasingly more vigorous physical activity for longer periods of time children could then achieve the silver and gold wristbands. The record sheets were then passed back to the university and they were analysed to explore differences in physical activity between groups of children. Physical activity was analysed by age, gender and parental occupation. This information was included on the record sheet.

Each of these primary schools also developed a network through which they produced a scheme of work on physical health. The plan was carefully sequenced to ensure progression in children's knowledge and skills. Children in the early years were taught how to clean their teeth and they participated in regular teeth cleaning sessions. They also learned about the importance of hand-washing. Children in Key Stage 1 and Key Stage 2 learned how to prepare and cook healthy food and how to analyse the calorific value of foods. Children in Key Stage 2 learned about bacteria and viruses and how to reduce the risk of infection. This supported the science curriculum. Children in Key Stage 2 also learned about allergies, immunisation and vaccination.

CRITICAL QUESTIONS

+ How might the physical health curriculum be structured to ensure progression in knowledge and skills?

+ The physical health curriculum may promote a lifestyle that conflicts with the lifestyles that children experience at home. How might you address this tension?

+ How might the school develop partnerships with local National Health Service organisations to support curriculum delivery?

DRUGS, ALCOHOL AND TOBACCO

A well-designed curriculum should introduce children to the dangers associated with smoking, alcohol use and drug taking. However, this curriculum needs to be age appropriate. It is also important to consider that some children will be living in households where these unhealthy behaviours are part of their everyday life. Some children, particularly as they reach Years 5 or 6, may have already started to experiment with these substances. Challenges may arise if children think that their family values are being criticised. It is important to handle this topic sensitively. Underpinning the teaching with scientific evidence that illustrates the dangers of substance misuse is one effective way of addressing this topic. Links can also be made to the warning signs that now appear on cigarettes and alcohol. There are many organisations and charities that work with children to support them to understand the risks associated with smoking and the consumption of drugs and alcohol. It is helpful to consider whether there are organisations or charities that can support this teaching within your own context. These programmes often strengthen current teaching as they may offer a different perspective to the one that a teacher is able to.

CRITICAL QUESTIONS

+ How might the substance misuse curriculum be structured to ensure progression in knowledge and skills?

+ The substance misuse curriculum may promote a lifestyle that conflicts with the lifestyles that children experience at home. How might you address this tension?

+ How might the school develop partnerships with local National Health Service organisations to support curriculum delivery?

BASIC FIRST AID

It is important that children understand how to make an efficient telephone call to the emergency services if this is required. The curriculum plays a crucial role in teaching children about the emergency services and the crucial contribution that these services make to society. Children must also understand some very basic first aid; for example, how to deal with simple injuries. It is important that schools ensure that staff delivering any training have suitable and appropriate qualifications and/or experience in relation to first aid. There are many organisations that offer programmes to support staff to deliver first aid training. Many of these organisations also offer programmes that train children to teach other children about basic approaches to first aid. This provides opportunities for children to take ownership of their skills and to work with their peers to develop and promote first aid. Primary schools can also work with parents to create opportunities for children to discuss their first aid skills. This allows children to develop their understanding of why first aid skills are important outside of the school environment.

CHANGING BODIES

As children move through Key Stage 2 they need to understand how the body changes from the age of 9 to 11 (ie, puberty). They also need to understand the emotional changes that may occur during this time and be prepared for some of the challenges associated with adolescence.

SUMMARY

This chapter has outlined the requirements of the statutory framework in relation to physical health and good mental well-being. It has explained the relationship between these while emphasising the importance of children being able to recognise and understand how they are different. It has highlighted the features of an effective curriculum in relation to physical health and mental well-being and some guidance has been offered to support your teaching and planning. Critical questions have been provided to support your reflection and some case study material has been offered to illuminate effective practice. The chapter has also explained the responsibility of schools to teach children about the benefits and risks associated with internet use and the concept of good citizenship has been explained. The chapter has also considered the role of the curriculum in supporting children to understand the dangers associated with smoking, alcohol use and drug taking. Finally, it has also outlined the role of schools in teaching children about basic first aid and the importance of sourcing adults with suitable qualifications and experience to deliver this training. The physical and emotional challenges associated with adolescence have also been identified.

FURTHER READING OR SOURCES OF FURTHER INFORMATION

Buhler, K (2000) *The Kids' Guide to First Aid: All About Bruises, Burns, Stings, Sprains & Other Ouches*. New York: Worthy Publishing.

Department for Education (DfE) (2019) *Teaching Online Safety in School*. London: DfE.

Health for Kids (nd) [online] Available at: www.healthforkids.co.uk (accessed 30 January 2020).

+ CHAPTER 7

SEX EDUCATION

CHAPTER OBJECTIVES

After reading this chapter you will understand:

+ the role of parental consultation when planning and delivering Sex Education;

+ how national curriculum science content supports the delivery of Sex Education;

+ your roles and responsibilities in relation to sensitivity and confidentiality;

+ how to establish clear rules and boundaries when delivering Sex Education;

+ the importance of teaching children about adolescence;

+ key considerations in relation to the teaching of reproduction;

+ how to support parents to discuss Sex Education;

+ school responsibilities and duties in relation to the Equality Act (2010).

INTRODUCTION

The statutory guidance (DfE, 2019a) does not make the teaching of Sex Education compulsory in primary schools but they can choose whether to teach it. Relationships Education is compulsory and the guidance for this already includes content on puberty and the changes that occur during adolescence. It is a matter for schools to decide what additional content to teach children if they choose to offer Sex Education. The statutory guidance states that Sex Education programmes should be tailored to the age and physical and emotional maturity of children in primary schools.

This chapter explores Sex Education and discusses the role of parental consultation for schools that decide to deliver this. It also highlights how the national curriculum science content supports the delivery of Sex Education. The chapter emphasises the importance of sensitivity and confidentiality for schools delivering Sex Education and it provides guidance on establishing clear rules and boundaries to support your teaching. It also offers guidance in relation to teaching children about adolescence and reproduction. Finally, some practical strategies are outlined to support parents to discuss Sex Education and the responsibilities and duties of schools are highlighted in relation to the Equality Act (2010).

CONSULTATION WITH PARENTS

If primary schools choose to provide Sex Education they must provide a policy for this which outlines the content of the Sex Education curriculum. Schools must specify the content which is additional to the content in the science national curriculum. Parents should be consulted about the subject content, particularly in relation to decisions about what constitutes 'age appropriate' content. In addition, the religious background of all pupils must be taken into account when designing the curriculum. Schools must ensure that they comply with the provisions of the Equality Act (2010) under which religion and/or belief are protected characteristics. The governors should not sanction the policy unless they are satisfied that a process of consultation has taken place with parents. It is good practice to provide a briefing event with parents and to allow them to preview any videos or other resources that you will use to support you teaching Sex Education.

CRITICAL QUESTIONS

+ How might religious perspectives or other beliefs influence people's views on Sex Education?

+ How would you develop a process of consultation with parents in relation to Sex Education?

+ Do you agree that Sex Education should be left to parents to address rather than schools? Justify your response to this question.

SUBJECT CONTENT

The national curriculum science content includes related subject content. Children in Key Stage 1 must be taught to:

+ *identify, name, draw and label the basic parts of the human body;*

+ *know that humans have offspring which grow into adults.*

In Key Stage 2 children must be able to:

+ *describe the human life cycle;*

+ *describe the changes as humans develop including the changes experienced in puberty;*

+ *describe the process of sexual reproduction in animals, including humans.*

(DfE, 2013)

SENSITIVITY

Teaching children about sex requires a great deal of sensitivity. A well-rounded Sex Education programme should help children to understand that sex is something which occurs within the context of loving relationships and even if this is not the case it should always take place between consenting adults. There may be children in the class who are being sexually abused or have been sexually abused in the past. They may not have previously realised that it is always wrong for an adult to engage in sexual activity with a child. Make it very clear to children that they can always talk to you privately if something is worrying them. It is essential that you are clear about the possibility that you may have to disclose the information to another adult to ensure the child's safety.

There may be children in the class who have had traumatic experiences, for example the death of a sibling during birth or prior to birth. Some children may have members of their family who have experienced sexual violence, including rape, and they may be aware of these experiences. Again, these experiences may be raised in class but it is always better to talk to children individually and privately about these very sensitive issues.

POST BOX

The use of a post box is a good strategy for children to ask you questions about sex. They can write down questions and remain anonymous. Make it very clear to children that you will not answer questions that are directed at you personally. Your sex life is not their business. You also retain the right to discard questions that you consider to be unsuitable or not age appropriate for the majority of the class. If children wish to talk to you individually they can indicate this to you by posting a message in the post box rather than having to approach you. It is then easy for you to initiate the discussion privately and sensitively. Children always need to be told that you cannot guarantee confidentiality and if you feel that they are at risk of harm then you have a legal obligation to inform the designated safeguarding lead (DSL).

ESTABLISHING RULES

Many children will find the topic of Sex Education embarrassing, particularly in the first lesson. It is a good idea to explain to children that this is perfectly normal and that most people find the topic of sex slightly embarrassing. Allow the children to laugh about it, then stop them, and explain that from now on you expect them to be mature and to treat the topic seriously. Children need to understand that you will not allow them to ask you personal questions and that you will not allow them to use inappropriate language in lessons. Insist that they use the correct scientific terminology for body parts right from the start. They should already know a variety of vocabulary from their science curriculum, including penis, vagina and breasts. Again, flag these words up in the first lesson, allow them to laugh about them and then explain that this is the last time you expect them to laugh. After all, they would not

79

laugh about the knee, arm and leg so there is no reason why they need to laugh when they hear the names of the genitals and other private body parts. Tell the children from the outset that personal questions directed at each other will not be tolerated. Explain to the children that sex is a private matter between consenting individuals who are legally allowed to have sex.

CRITICAL QUESTIONS

+ What additional content might primary schools want to include in a Sex Education policy?

+ What is meant by an age appropriate Sex Education curriculum?

+ When and how should Sex Education content be introduced in primary schools?

+ What factors might influence children's sexual awareness?

PREPARING FOR ADOLESCENCE

Children need to understand how their bodies will physically change, particularly from the age of 9 to 11, including physical and emotional changes. Children need to understand puberty within the human life cycle. In addition, pupils should know about menstrual well-being, including key facts about the menstrual cycle. This content is already addressed in the statutory guidance for Health Education. Menstruation can be confusing and distressing for girls if they are not aware of it before it happens. Pupils therefore need to understand what an average period entails, the range of menstrual products that are available and the implications of menstruation for emotional and physical health. Schools need to help girls prepare for and manage menstruation, including with requests for menstrual products.

CRITICAL QUESTIONS

+ What aspects of Sex Education should be covered in primary schools?

+ What aspects of Sex Education are not appropriate for primary schools and should only be taught in secondary schools?

REPRODUCTION

The process of human sexual reproduction is covered in the science national curriculum. It is important that subject content is age appropriate and that parents are fully aware of the content that is being taught. Equally, it is important for schools to consider carefully how subject content will be taught as well as what is taught.

SUPPORTING PARENTS

Parents may benefit from clear guidance on how to handle difficult questions from their child about sex. Sadly, too many parents leave their children to learn about Sex Education in the school playground because they find it too embarrassing to discuss with their child. Guidance on how to have conversations about sex, what resources to use and how to answer difficult questions may be extremely valuable for parents who find this a tricky topic to raise. Some schools run parental workshops to develop their confidence in addressing sex with their child.

THE PARENTAL RIGHT TO WITHDRAW

Parents do not have a right to withdraw their child from Relationships Education. However, they do have a right to withdraw their child from Sex Education in both primary and secondary schools. The right to withdraw should be clearly stated in the RSE policy.

RELIGION AND SEX EDUCATION

Schools are required by law to meet their legal duties in relation to the Equality Act (2010). This includes acknowledging religious perspectives (and people with other beliefs) on relationships and sex.

The RSE framework states:

All schools may teach about faith perspectives. In particular, schools with a religious character may teach the distinctive faith perspective on relationships, and balanced debate may take place about issues that are seen as contentious.

(DfE, 2019a, p 12)

CRITICAL QUESTIONS

+ What are your views on all schools teaching children about faith perspectives on relationships and sex?

+ What issues may arise from the statement 'schools with a religious character may teach the distinctive faith perspective on relationships'?

CASE STUDY

HUMAN LIFE CYCLE

YEAR 2, SCIENCE

In the programmes of study for Year 2 science, children need to know that animals, including humans, have offspring which grow into adults. This lesson provides an example of how you might address this.

+ Show the children photographs of an adult, a baby, a toddler, an adolescent, a middle-aged person and an older person.

+ Ask the children to order the photographs along a timeline to demonstrate the stages of life.

+ Ask the children to tell you where babies come from.

+ Explain that humans have babies through a process called reproduction. Introduce the word 'offspring'.

+ Explain that other animals also reproduce.

+ Send the children to tables and ask them to work in pairs. Provide each pair with separate photographs of adult animals and baby animals. Ask them to match the animal with the correct offspring.

+ Ask the children to identify the names of the offspring. Give each pair some cards with offspring vocabulary and vocabulary for adult animals. Ask them to place the words next to the correct offspring and adults.

+ Explain to the children that offspring can resemble the adults in many ways, including physical features. However, explain that human offspring rarely look identical to their parents even though they will share some of their physical characteristics.

+ Explain that the adult produces the offspring and then the offspring grows and turns into an adult and may produce their own offspring through reproduction. This is how life continues to exist.

CASE STUDY

REPRODUCTION

YEAR 5, SCIENCE

In the programmes of study for Year 5 science, children need to understand sexual reproduction. This lesson will introduce this concept to children.

Prior learning

+ The children will have been taught the names of the genitals.

+ The children will have been introduced to the internal parts of the vagina and the penis and produced labelled diagrams.

+ The children will have watched this video on sexual reproduction in plants and animals: www.twinkl.co.uk/teaching-wiki/sexual-reproduction (accessed 30 January 2020).

Lesson content

+ Remind the children that in Year 2 they learned about reproduction and offspring.

+ Explain that in this lesson they will learn about sexual reproduction.

+ Explain that sexual reproduction usually, but not always, occurs through the process of sexual intercourse.

+ Use videos, cartoons and diagrams to explain the process of sexual reproduction.

+ Remind the children of the names of the reproductive organs and explain the process of fertilisation of the ovum by the sperm. This is more effective when it is supported by a video or diagrams.

+ Introduce the children to pregnancy.

CRITICAL QUESTIONS

+ What might you say to a child at the point that a sensitive issue is raised during the lesson?

+ How might you follow up sensitive issues with specific children after the lesson?

SUMMARY

This chapter has explored Sex Education and has discussed the role of parental consultation for schools that decide to deliver this. It has also highlighted how the national curriculum science content supports the delivery of Sex Education. The chapter has emphasised the importance of sensitivity and confidentiality for schools delivering Sex Education and it has provided guidance on establishing clear rules and boundaries to support your teaching. It has also offered guidance in relation to teaching children about adolescence and reproduction. Finally, some practical strategies have been outlined to support parents to discuss Sex Education and the responsibilities and duties of schools have been highlighted in relation to the Equality Act (2010). Throughout the chapter some case study material has been provided to illuminate effective practice and critical questions have been offered to support your reflection.

FURTHER READING OR SOURCES OF FURTHER INFORMATION

PANTS Resources for Schools and Teachers. Available at: https://learning.nspcc.org.uk/research-resources/schools/pants-teaching/ (accessed 4 February 2020).

Rise Above for Schools. Available at: https://campaignresources.phe.gov.uk/schools/topics/rise-above/overview?WT.mc_id=RiseAboveforSchools_PSHEA_EdComs_Resource_listing_Sep17#dealing-with-change (accessed 4 February 2020).

The Voice of Sex Education in England. Available at: www.sexeducationforum.org.uk/ (accessed 4 February 2020).

Parents and SRE: A Sex Education Forum Evidence Briefing. Available at: www.sexeducationforum.org.uk/sites/default/files/field/attachment/SRE%20and%20parents%20-%20evidence%20-%202011.pdf (accessed 4 February 2020).

✚ CHAPTER 8

RELATIONSHIPS EDUCATION FOR VULNERABLE LEARNERS

CHAPTER OBJECTIVES

After reading this chapter you will understand:

+ how to support children with SEND to establish and develop relationships;

+ how to meet the needs of children with LGBT identities;

+ the difficulties that children living in care may experience when establishing secure, trusting relationships.

INTRODUCTION

Children of the same age might be developmentally at different stages. Teaching methods should therefore take into account children's different needs, particularly in relation to those with Special Educational Needs and Disabilities (SEND). The statutory framework for Relationships Education (DfE, 2019a) advises schools to take into account these needs by adopting flexible modes of delivery. Some children may need a specific programme which is tailored to meet their needs, some delivery might take place in small groups and some delivery might take place with the whole class. This chapter addresses the relationship education needs of children with SEND, those who identify as LGBT and children who are looked after.

LEGISLATION

The Equality Act (2010) sets out the legal obligations that schools must meet in relation to children with disabilities. The main legal duties of schools are listed below:

+ Schools must not directly or indirectly discriminate against, harass or victimise disabled children and young people.

+ Schools must make reasonable adjustments to ensure that children with disabilities are not at a substantial disadvantage compared with their peers.

+ The Public Sector Equality Duty states that schools must foster good relations between children who have a disability and those who do not.

Schools must therefore ensure that children with SEND receive their entitlement to a Relationships Education curriculum. They must ensure that children with disabilities and those without disabilities are supported to establish healthy relationships. This will help to ensure that children with SEND are not subjected to discrimination. They have the same right to enjoy relationships as all children do. If they do not have the necessary skills required to establish healthy relationships, the Relationships Education curriculum should support them to develop these skills so that they can experience the benefits of relationships. A tailored curriculum which focuses on developing relationship skills could constitute a reasonable adjustment in relation to the equality legislation.

COMMUNICATION AND INTERACTION NEEDS

Some children with SEND have specific difficulties with establishing relationships. Children with speech, language and communication needs, including children who stammer, are particularly vulnerable to being bullied because of their difficulties. They may develop low self esteem and this can impact on their ability to form relationships with others. As a result of low self esteem, they may not develop self respect, which is critical for relationship building. They may also lack confidence in seeking relationships because of their language and communication difficulties. Developing self esteem and understanding of self respect are essential so that children with communication and interaction needs can build healthy relationships. In addition, other children may need support in understanding how to communicate with children with communication and interaction needs. One way of supporting this is for all children to learn sign language so that they can effectively communicate and build relationships with children who are non-verbal. In addition, all children can be taught how to use pictures, signs and symbols to facilitate communication with children who are non-verbal. To support children who stammer, all children need to understand the importance of demonstrating patience when they communicate with children who have this difficulty and also the importance of not finishing sentences for them. Teaching all children how to effectively communicate with children with speech, language and communication needs will support the development of healthy relationships.

Children who are identified with Autistic Spectrum Conditions (ASC) typically have three main areas of difficulty which can impact on their ability to form relationships. They often experience difficulties with social interaction, social communication and rigidity of thought.

Children with ASC may find social interaction difficult. Some will find it difficult to work with others in pairs and small groups and this can make it difficult for them to establish relationships. It is important to recognise that children with ASC are individuals. Some will have greater capacity for social interaction than others and some will find any social interaction distressing. Difficulties with social communication may mean that children with ASC struggle to understand the rules of social communication. They might struggle to maintain eye contact and with turn-taking and the use of non-verbal cues to support verbal nteractions.

In addition, they might struggle to understand the 'backwards and for-wards' nature of communication. Fundamentally, the key area of diffi-culty lies in communication rather than language. Difficulties in social communication can mean that children with autism struggle to estab-lish relationships. Rigid thought processes can be evident, which result in a desire for consistency and clear routines. When routines change, this can result in distress which can impact on their behaviour. Peers need to understand the potential triggers for specific behaviours and respond to them with patience and empathy.

In addition to these key areas of difficulty, children with autism struggle to demonstrate empathy towards others. They lack a theory of mind. This means that they may fail to respond to others with empathy when people are distressed. They may also make inappropriate but literal comments about others because they struggle to understand how their words and actions can impact on other people. Difficulties with demonstrating empathy towards others can affect their capacity to form relationships with peers, particularly if they demonstrate socially inappropriate behaviour.

Children with social, emotional and mental health needs may also find it difficult to establish relationships. Peers may interpret their behav-iour as negative and socially undesirable and they may choose not to interact with them. Children's unmet needs are often reflected through their behaviours. Many children with poor behaviour have experienced trauma, parental conflict, abuse and neglect. Often their basic needs are not met and they may have poor self esteem. Their difficulties may arise from not forming secure attachments with their primary care-giver. Children living in areas of social deprivation are more likely to experience mental ill health and children who are looked after or those who identify as LGBT are more at risk of developing mental ill health.

Children with mild and specific learning difficulties may also experi-ence difficulties establishing secure relationships due to low self esteem and low confidence. Children of the same age may be devel-opmentally at different stages and this can impact on their readiness for Relationships Education. Children with physical, hearing or visual impairments may also experience poor self esteem which can detrimen-tally impact on their capacities to establish effective relationships with others. Children with profound and multiple learning disabilities have complex difficulties that can impact detrimentally on their capacity to secure relationships with others.

CRITICAL QUESTIONS

+ Is the guidance in the statutory framework for Relationships Education adequate to support teachers to provide Relationships Education for children with SEND?

+ How can schools best provide Relationships Education for children with SEND?

CASE STUDY

RELATIONSHIPS EDUCATION FOR CHILDREN WITH AUTISM

YEARS 1 AND 2, PSHE

A school identified a small group of children with Autistic Spectrum Conditions who they felt would benefit from a social and emotional regulation intervention programme.

The sessions were carefully structured and spanned two terms. The children were initially taught about different feelings. Each lesson focused on one feeling. Over the duration of the intervention several feelings were introduced. This included happiness, sadness, frustration, jealously, excitement, anger and feeling scared. The children were introduced to the feelings through stories and they were taught strategies for regulating their feelings. In addition, the sessions supported the children to learn how to recognise feelings in other people and to respond appropriately to others when specific emotions were demonstrated. For example, they learned how to support another child who was feeling upset.

Some of the sessions focused on teaching the children the skills of social communication. These included:

+ turn-taking;

+ building on what another person has said within a conversation;

+ affirming what other people are saying to them through nodding and smiling, etc;

+ use of gesture within conversation;

+ sticking to a topic.

The children were given opportunities to practise these skills through role-play in pairs. The children were taught to differentiate between socially desirable and socially undesirable comments. They were taught to understand how their words and actions can affect other people, even if they are not intending to upset someone by making literal comments. For example, they learned that telling a person that they are fat may be an accurate description but it is not socially acceptable because this can make someone feel sad.

By the end of the programme the children were able to recognise a range of emotions. They were more able to regulate their feelings and their responses to other people. These skills enabled them to establish better relationships with their peers.

COGNITION AND LEARNING NEEDS

Children with cognition and learning needs form a diverse group. Needs may range from moderate learning difficulties (MLDs) to profound and multiple learning difficulties (PMLDs). Some children may also have specific learning difficulties such as dyslexia, dyscalculia and dyspraxia (SpLDs).

It is important to consider carefully the needs of children within this group. Some children with cognition and learning needs may be operating at an earlier stage of cognitive development than the majority of their peers of the same age. The Relationships Education curriculum for these children will therefore need to be age appropriate.

Children with cognition and learning needs are vulnerable to exploitation within relationships. The curriculum should therefore help them to recognise when relationships are making them feel unhappy or unsafe. They need to be taught to recognise coercion, manipulation and other forms of abuse so that they can identify these if they occur. In addition, they also need to know how to report their concerns to other people, how to access support and who to talk to if they feel that they are being abused.

Some children with cognition and learning needs will have low self esteem. Their view of themselves (self concept) will be informed by the views that others have of them including peers and adults. If other people demonstrate negative views towards them, they may start to internalise these views and develop a poor self concept. Their self esteem is also influenced by their self efficacy. Self efficacy is their perception of their own competence. As a result of their cognition and learning needs there is a risk that they may start to develop a negative view of their own competence. This will impact negatively on their self esteem. If they start to develop low self esteem there is also a risk that they will not develop self respect. They may start to feel that they are not a good enough person and therefore not worthy of other people's respect. Therefore, it is essential that children learn through the Relationships Education curriculum that they are worthy of self respect and that they have a right to expect this from others. A well-designed Relationships Education curriculum for children with cognition and learning needs should therefore focus on developing children's self esteem and their understanding of self respect. As their self esteem develops, this should support them in recognising that they have a right to self respect, although self respect may need to be explicitly taught.

Children with cognition and learning needs may also need to learn that their body belongs to them and that other people should not touch their body without permission. As they may be vulnerable to abuse it is critical that they understand that other people are not entitled to invade their personal space or touch their body without their permission. Additionally, it is critical for them to understand that they should not touch other people's bodies without permission and that they should not invade other people's personal space. Some children with cognition and learning needs will seek other people's affection physically by touching other people. These children need to understand that although some forms of touch are acceptable, other forms of touch are unacceptable and they may therefore need to be taught about more appropriate ways of greeting people. A simple example is to teach them to greet others using a handshake rather than a hug. This prevents them from invading other people's personal space and also minimises the risk that they might be abused.

Children with cognition and learning needs may find it difficult to develop relationships with others. A range of factors contribute to this, including the fact that they might be operating at an earlier stage of cognitive development than their same-age peers. The character traits that support people to effectively build relationships may also need to explicitly be taught through modelling. These include truthfulness, trust, loyalty, kindness, generosity, respect, courtesy and manners. Children with cognition and learning needs may need a carefully designed structured programme of character education that systematically enables children to learn about these important character traits, which will help them to establish secure, healthy relationships.

They may also need access to a social and emotional curriculum. Social and emotional understanding is crucial for healthy relationships. Children need to develop their understanding of the rules of social communication. These include turn-taking, eye contact, gesture, knowing when to take pauses and building on what other people have said in conversation. Children also need to understand how to adapt their behaviour in different social contexts. Healthy friendships are also underpinned by emotional literacy. Emotional literacy enables people to recognise feelings in others and demonstrate empathy towards others when they need support. Emotional literacy also enables children to recognise and name their own feelings and to regulate these feelings. Emotional and social regulation within relationships prevents situations from becoming volatile and helps individuals to understand the impact that their words and actions might have on other people. Children with cognition and learning needs may need an explicit social and emotional curriculum which supports them in learning about social norms and behaviour, helps them to recognise and name feelings and supports them to regulate their social and emotional behaviours.

To support children with cognition and learning needs to develop healthy relationships, all children need to understand the importance of respecting others regardless of their differences. This theme of respect is something that will need to be constantly revisited. If children understand the importance of this then it will reduce the likelihood of children with cognition and learning needs being exploited or abused within relationships.

SOCIAL, EMOTIONAL AND MENTAL HEALTH NEEDS

Children with social, emotional and mental health needs are a diverse group that includes children with behavioural needs but also children with more specific mental health needs.

Behaviour is usually an attempt by the child to communicate an unmet need. Children may demonstrate specific undesirable behaviours for a range of reasons and these behaviours can impact on their ability to establish healthy relationships with others. Unacceptable behaviour can originate from low self esteem, poor attachments with parents, experience of abuse, neglect, rejection and trauma. In addition, some unacceptable behaviours may have been modelled in the family or community contexts. Children with social, emotional and mental health needs may struggle to establish relationships because they may have experienced, or be experiencing, unhealthy relationships in their families and communities. They may have been let down by others in relationships and they might not trust other people. Other children may also be reluctant to establish relationships with them due to their complex needs. They may need a tailored Relationships Education curriculum through which they learn:

+ the value of healthy human relationships;
+ the character traits that will support them in establishing healthy relationships;
+ emotional literacy and regulation;
+ social behaviour and regulation;
+ self respect;
+ how others can be a source of support;
+ how to seek help if relationships are unhealthy;
+ to develop their self esteem.

Mental health needs may arise from children's experiences of unhealthy relationships. These negative experiences may have led them to believe that unhealthy relationships are typical of all relationships and that they do not deserve self respect. Through Relationships Education children can start to understand the difference between healthy and unhealthy relationships. They can start to understand that they deserve respect from others and they can learn how to report abuse when they experience it. As children learn about the characteristics of unhealthy relationships, they may have to reframe their understanding of relationships, particularly if they have been exposed to unhealthy relationships in other contexts. Children's social backgrounds should not define what they become. Through the Relationships Education curriculum children can learn to critically evaluate the previous relationships that they have established, particularly if those relationships have been unhealthy and resulted in them developing social, emotional and mental health needs.

CASE STUDY

SOLUTION-FOCUSED APPROACHES

YEAR 4, PSHE

A school adopted solution-focused approaches to support the development of children's self esteem and behaviour. Solution-focused strategies can be useful to help children set goals. The school implemented the following approaches for children who demonstrated the most challenging behaviour.

+ Problem-free talk: talk about what they are good at, what they enjoy and their interests.

+ Exception finding: talk about the exceptions to their usual behaviour; for example, when they stayed calm in a difficult situation.

+ Complimenting: notice when they do something well and compliment them for it.

+ Scaling: ask them to scale their behaviour/confidence/motivation/ mood/self worth, etc on a scale from 1 to 10 (negative to positive). Then ask them to justify why they have selected a specific number by supporting them to describe what they can do rather than what they cannot do (example: *So why have you given yourself a 2 for behaviour? That means you are doing something right. So, what can you do?*). Then ask them to set a goal (*Where on the scale will you be next term? What will you be doing differently? How will I know you have moved up the scale?*). This supports them to set themselves realistic goals.

SENSORY NEEDS

Sensory needs include visual impairment, hearing impairment and multisensory impairment. The complex needs of these children may mean that they develop low self esteem, which can detrimentally impact on their ability to form relationships. Their needs can also prevent other children from establishing relationships with them. A key aim of Relationships Education is for children to learn to respect people's differences. Children with sensory needs may need a tailored programme through which they learn to develop their self esteem and their understanding of self respect. Strategies to support children with sensory impairment for building relationships are listed below:

+ introduce a programme to develop self esteem;

+ teach about the importance of self respect;

+ teach all children strategies to facilitate communication with children with sensory needs, including sign language;

+ teach all children about the importance of respecting others irrespective of differences;

+ provide children with a sensory need with a 'buddy' who can support them, particularly during playtimes;

+ introduce 'circle of friends';

+ teach all children to assess risk particularly for children with visual impairment who may be at risk of injury.

CIRCLE OF FRIENDS

This is a strategy which is useful to enhance the self esteem of children with a wide range of SEND. It will support them in developing positive friendships. In this approach a small group of children are selected to form a friendship group around a child with a specific SEND. The group take responsibility for noticing things that the child has done well each week. The group meet weekly and communicate with the child all their successes. This helps the child to develop a secure friendship group and it also supports the development of their self esteem.

PHYSICAL NEEDS

Children with physical needs may need specific support in developing relationships. Their physical needs may mean that they have restricted mobility and they may therefore not have the same agility as their peers. They may find it more challenging to participate in some of the games that their peers play and they may have developed low self esteem as a result of their needs. It is therefore important, first and foremost, to focus on developing their self esteem so that they are more confident in establishing relationships with others. It is also important to teach all children to respect differences and to suggest ways that they can include children with physical needs into games and other activities. Developing social connectivity is vital for good mental health and the Relationships Education should therefore be designed to support all children to develop healthy friendships.

Some children with physical needs may be vulnerable to bullying. A well-designed Relationships Education curriculum should therefore ensure that these children can identify the characteristics of unhealthy relationships and that they know how to report their concerns to others. All children need to be taught to recognise bullying within relationships so that they can take action if this occurs.

It is also possible that children with physical needs have been protected from danger within the context of their families and communities. However, all children need to be encouraged to take safe risks. They need to be able to identify and manage risks so that they can experience equality of opportunity. Risk will be presented within the context of friendships, particularly when children with physical needs play with other children. All children therefore need to understand the concepts of safe and unsafe risks within relationships. It might be extremely dangerous for a child with physical needs to participate in specific types of play, but through Relationships Education children can learn how to adapt activities to ensure that all children can participate safely in an activity.

Some children with physical needs may not have experience of developing relationships with their peers due to parental concerns about their safety. They might not have the same opportunities to meet other children socially outside school and they might not participate in co-curricular activities, particularly if their parents are concerned that specific activities may present risks. A well-rounded education supports children to develop social relationships. Social relationships improve overall well-being and foster a sense of belonging within school. Children who have less experience of establishing relationships may therefore need additional support in developing their social and emotional literacy and regulatory skills so that they can form healthy relationships with others. In addition, they may benefit from a structured programme that systematically introduces them to positive character traits which should be demonstrated within the context of relationships.

MEETING THE NEEDS OF LGBT PUPILS

Children in primary school may be LGBT but they may not have the vocabulary to describe how they feel. In addition, even if they do have the vocabulary, they may not be willing to disclose their sexual orientation or gender identity at this point until they have had time to come to terms with it themselves.

Regardless of this, homophobic, biphobic and transphobic bullying in school is caused by gender stereotypes and prejudice. Children who do not conform to gender norms are at risk of being subjected to prejudice-based bullying, irrespective of their sexuality. Boys who do not like sports and prefer to play with girls are at risk of being bullied. Girls who do not play with dolls but prefer to play football with boys are also at risk of being bullied. These children may experience isolation simply because their choices and mannerisms do not reflect typical gender norms.

To support children to develop effective relationships, all primary schools should provide a curriculum that addresses gender stereotypes. This curriculum should be taught to all pupils. In addition, all primary schools should provide a programme of Relationships Education which addresses:

+ LGBT identities;

+ LGBT relationships;

+ same-sex marriage;

+ homophobic, biphobic and transphobic bullying.

It is never too early for children to start learning that LGBT people exist (Glazzard and Stones, 2019). Children of all ages will know LGBT people and may have same-sex parents. They may know LGBT people in their families or communities. The earlier children start to learn about this aspect of diversity, the more likely it is that schools can foster the development of inclusive values within children. A curriculum that promotes LGBT inclusion prepares children for life in modern Britain. In addition, it addresses the requirements of the Equality Act (2010).

USING TEXTS

There is a rich range of children's story books now that reflect LGBT identities. Some of these stories reflect same-sex parents and others portray same-sex relationships through 'animal' families. There are also a range of stories that challenge traditional gender stereotypes. Challenging traditional assumptions about gender is important because boys and girls who do not conform to gender stereotypes become targets of homophobic, biphobic and transphobic bullying regardless of whether they identify as LGBT. It is therefore important that young children are exposed to stories that portray girls and women as strong and powerful. Equally, it is important that stories portray boys as sensitive and caring. Children develop stereotypes about the kind of activities that boys and girls are 'supposed' to participate in and those who do not like gender-typical activities can become victims of homophobic, biphobic and transphobic bullying. It is important that stories portray boys involved in activities such as dancing and cooking and that male adults are portrayed in caring roles. Stories should also portray boys and girls wearing clothes that do not conform to their gender stereotype. Stories that depict girls engaging in activities which are traditionally associated with boys should also be used as well as stories which portray females in roles that are traditionally associated with females.

WORKING WITH PARENTS

Before starting any work on LGBT identities and experiences in primary schools, it is important that you consult with parents. This is particularly important if you are working in a faith school or if the school is situated in a strong religious community. Parents will need to understand:

+ why this work is important and how it supports the Equality Act (2010);
+ what is being taught;
+ the resources that are being used.

Parents will need reassurance that the school is not promoting a particular sexual orientation or gender identity and that none of the teaching will address sex. Parents do not have the right to withdraw children from lessons that address LGBT issues.

WHY DO PARENTS OBJECT TO PROMOTING LGBT INCLUSION?

Often it is the fear of parental backlash that prevents schools from addressing this strand of inclusion. Often, this fear is unfounded, and many schools do manage to address this work without any parental complaints.

When parents do complain, it is usually from a position that is uninformed. Parents may be worried that the school is attempting to promote a lesbian, gay, bisexual or transgender identity in young children. They may also be worried that the lessons will address sex. These fears are based on lack of understanding of what is being taught and sometimes they are based on prejudice.

In primary schools the focus of all teaching is about relationships. Children need to recognise that some people have same-sex parents and that they love their children in the same way that heterosexual parents love their children. Children need to know that LGBT people exist. They exist in school and in families and communities. They also exist in all countries and people with LGBT identities can also be religious. By focusing on the facts, lessons contribute to the knowledge-rich curriculum which is now so important in schools.

Through learning about different kinds of relationships, children will be able to make sense of the relationships that are naturally part of their lives, schools, families and communities. None of the teaching in schools should promote a particular identity or way of life, including heterosexual identities.

DEVELOP A WORKING GROUP

One strategy is to develop a working group which includes parents, staff and governors. The group can co-construct the LGBT curriculum. If your school is following a published scheme, the group can review this. The working group can also make decisions on how to address LGBT inclusion through the curriculum and consider how key celebrations will be addressed. Examples include local Pride events and LGBT history month.

MAKE IT VISIBLE

As the work progresses in school, you should seek opportunities to share successes with parents. You may wish to consider posting some of the curriculum projects on a school blog so that parents can read about what their children are learning. You might also wish to create displays of the work so that children's achievements are also visible.

ADDRESS PARENTAL COMPLAINTS

It can be very unsettling for schools, and particularly for teachers, when parents make complaints. Teachers must be allowed to teach lessons without experiencing additional and unnecessary stress that may arise from dealing with parental complaints. The LGBT inclusion lead or a member of the senior leadership team should address all parental complaints and therefore act as a buffer for teachers and other staff.

Nevertheless, parental complaints still have to be addressed. It is important to invite parents in for a meeting and to listen to their concerns. Thank them for taking the time to come and see you and ask them to talk through their concerns. Maintain eye contact, smile and jot down a few notes as they talk to you. Then address systematically each point they have raised. Reiterate the school's legal duties under the Public Sector Equality Duty and the legal duties of schools under the Equality Act (2010) to ensure that protected groups do not experience discrimination. Emphasise that the lesson content focuses on gender stereotypes, different identities and inclusive relationships. Explain to parents that it is a legal duty of schools to teach children to respect all types of diversity.

In these meetings, be prepared to share schemes of work, lesson plans and resources that are being used in different year groups to reassure parents that teachers are not teaching about sex and not promoting a specific sexual orientation or gender identity.

EXPLORING THE CHALLENGES

Parents with strong religious beliefs may be concerned about the following.

+ The LGBT curriculum will promote homosexuality or bisexuality as a way of life.

+ The teaching of transgender identities does not align with religious values.

+ Lessons will address same-sex marriage.

+ The teaching of LGBT issues will also cover sex in same-sex relationships.

+ The curriculum will not align with the values of the faith.

101

Each of these issues is now addressed below.

THE LGBT CURRICULUM WILL PROMOTE HOMOSEXUALITY OR BISEXUALITY AS A WAY OF LIFE

A curriculum that focuses on LGBT inclusion does not attempt to promote homosexuality or bisexuality. The purpose of the curriculum is to teach children that LGBT people exist within society, that there are different types of relationships and that same-sex people can marry. Children will not become gay, lesbian or bisexual through being exposed to a curriculum that addresses these identities. Although the religion may not permit these identities, children will be exposed to different identities and a broad range of relationships in different social contexts. They will meet LGBT people at school, in college, in communities, at university and in the world of work. It is therefore critical that they are aware of these identities and are able to demonstrate respect towards people who are different.

Although the religion may not agree with LGBT identities, same-sex relationships or same-sex marriage, it is important that parents understand that all primary schools are required to teach the fundamental British values and one of these values is the rule of law. This is specified in the Teachers' Standards (DfE, 2013). Schools are therefore required to teach children about the law of the land, irrespective of religious beliefs.

In addition, schools are also required to comply with the duties that are stipulated in the Equality Act (2010) including Section 149 of the Equality Act, the Public Sector Equality Duty. The Equality Act (2010) places a legal duty on schools to protect LGBT people from direct and indirect forms of discrimination. Protection from direct discrimination can be achieved through addressing homophobic, biphobic and transphobic bullying. Schools must not introduce rules that will place an individual at a disadvantage. This could include a uniform policy which unfairly discriminates against a transgender child. This is an example of indirect discrimination. The Public Sector Equality Duty places a legal duty on schools to promote good relations between different groups of people.

Parents with strong religious beliefs must be supported to understand that non-normative identities will be taught but not promoted. Schools must make their legal obligations very clear to parents so that parents understand the legal rationale for this work.

THE TEACHING OF TRANSGENDER IDENTITIES DOES NOT ALIGN WITH RELIGIOUS VALUES

It is important to emphasise to parents that you are not promoting transgender identities as a way of life because people do not choose to be transgender. The purpose of the LGBT curriculum is to teach children that people who are transgender exist, that they have a right to be respected and a legal right under the Equality Act (2010) to be free from discrimination. Schools have a legal responsibility to promote good relations between different groups of people and this extends to transgender. Young people will meet transgender people in society, in places of study and in places of work and they need to learn to treat them with respect and to positively affirm their identity. You can acknowledge to parents that although you understand that transgender identities may not be accepted in their faith, people in Britain are able by law to go through a process of gender reassignment. It is the responsibility of schools to teach children about the rule of law even though you recognise that it might not be accepted within their faith.

LESSONS WILL ADDRESS SAME-SEX MARRIAGE

Parents need to understand that schools must teach children about the rule of law. In the United Kingdom it is legal for people of the same sex to marry and therefore schools must teach this. You can acknowledge to parents that this may not be allowed within the context of a specific religion, but the role of schools is to teach children the law in the United Kingdom. Children may also have friends in school who have same-sex parents, so teaching them about same-sex marriage enables them to understand the backgrounds and circumstances of their peers.

THE TEACHING OF LGBT ISSUES WILL ALSO COVER SEX IN SAME-SEX RELATIONSHIPS

You will need to explain to parents that in primary schools children are never taught about sex within the context of same-sex relationships. The focus of the teaching is on identities and Relationships Education.

103

THE CURRICULUM WILL NOT ALIGN WITH THE VALUES OF THE FAITH

You may need to acknowledge to parents that the values of the religion may not support LGBT identities or same-sex marriage. At the same time, you may also need to point out that the teaching of LGBT identities and experiences in primary schools supports the Equality Act (2010), the Public Sector Equality Duty and fundamental British values (ie, the rule of law). You can also explain to parents that Ofsted routinely monitors the extent of homophobic, biphobic and transphobic bullying during school inspections and therefore it is critical that schools are addressing this as a priority.

BUILDING RELATIONSHIPS

Before you begin any curriculum work on LGBT inclusion it is important to invite parents into school to attend a meeting. At this meeting you should:

+ Explain to parents why the school needs to address this strand of inclusion.
+ Explain the content that will be covered in lessons. Show parents examples of the resources that will be used.
+ Emphasise that the curriculum will not promote specific sexualities or gender identities.
+ Emphasise that the focus of the content is on Relationships Education.

It is important that parents clearly understand why this work is crucial:

+ Schools are legally obliged to address the Equality Act (2010) and the requirement to promote good relations between different groups of people as well as the need to protect LGBT children from discrimination, bullying or harassment.
+ Schools are legally required to teach fundamental British values, including the law. In the United Kingdom it is lawful for LGBT people to exist and it is lawful to enter into same-sex marriage. Children need to be taught the law, regardless of faith values.

Explain to parents that you wish the meeting to be calm and respectful. Acknowledge that the parents may have strong religious values and acknowledge that some of the things that are being taught will conflict with faith values. However, explain to the parents that the children will be taught this also. For example, in some lessons teachers may use phrases such as: *'Same-sex marriage is not allowed in your religion, but it is allowed in British law.'* Emphasise to parents that the lesson content will not cover sex within the context of same-sex relationships and that no lessons will promote a specific sexual orientation or gender identity.

Being honest with parents will help to build their trust. It is important that you listen to their concerns, that you demonstrate that you value and understand their religious beliefs and that you provide them with an opportunity to offer feedback. You may need to be prepared to 'meet in the middle' with parents in order to prevent parental backlash from occurring.

ESTABLISHING TRUST

It is crucial that you establish parental trust. To establish trust:

+ Agree with them how you will address this strand of inclusion.
+ Make assurances that lessons will not promote a sexual orientation or gender identity.
+ Keep them fully informed about curriculum developments.
+ Be open to further meetings with parents to discuss their concerns.

CASE STUDY

LGBT INCLUSION

YEAR 6, PSHE/ENGLISH

In this unit of work the children were taught a series of lessons that were designed to promote LGBT inclusion. These were structured as follows.

Lesson 1

The children were introduced to the concept of stereotypes. They were asked to identify the stereotypes associated with being a boy and those associated with being a girl. They were then asked to consider the harmful effects of stereotypes including bullying, isolation and reduced confidence and self esteem. The children were provided with a mixture of facts and stereotypes associated with gender and they were asked to sort them into these two groups.

Lesson 2

The children were introduced to homophobic, biphobic and transphobic bullying. They were taught about the Equality Act (2010). They were taught about what constitutes a homophobic, biphobic and transphobic incident. They were also taught about the link between gender stereotypes (introduced in the previous lesson) and prejudice-based bullying. The children were asked to make posters to be displayed around the school to inform the school community about homophobic, biphobic and transphobic bullying.

Lesson 3

The school made a link with a national LGBT charity. The charity deploys LGBT young people to go into schools to talk to the children about their own experiences of homophobic, biphobic and transphobic bullying and to showcase their achievements despite their experiences of bullying. The children listened to a presentation by an LGBT young person and watched age appropriate videos that addressed homophobic, biphobic and transphobic bullying.

Lesson 4

The children were introduced to the concept of bystanders. The teacher explained that observing bullying and not reporting it is inappropriate because it allows the perpetrator(s) to continue with bullying behaviour without being challenged. The teacher explained that observing bullying and not reporting it is just as bad as the person who is carrying out the bullying. The victims rely on the people who observe the bullying to report it so that action can be taken to stop the bullying from continuing. The children were asked to identify ways of responding to bullying if they observe it.

Lesson 5

In this lesson the children were introduced to the concept of micro-aggressions that can occur within relationships and classrooms. Micro-aggressions are subtle forms of bullying and usually involve non-verbal forms of bullying. The teacher provided the children with a few examples of micro-aggressions and then played a video to show examples of micro-aggressions in action. The teacher then provided the children with scenarios that included micro-aggressions, verbal bullying, physical bullying and cyberbullying. In pairs the children read the scenarios and had to decide which type of bullying each represented. The children were required to justify their responses using a written explanation.

Lesson 6

This lesson focused on same-sex marriage. The teacher introduced the children to the purpose of marriage and explained that traditionally marriage has taken place between a woman and a man. The teacher then introduced same-sex marriage to the children. The teacher explained about the significance of the Marriage Act in 2013. It was emphasised that same-sex marriage is now legal in the UK. The teacher explained the difference between a marriage and a civil partnership and explained that marriage or civil partnership is a protected characteristic in the Equality Act (2010). The children were then asked to plan a factsheet (non-chronological report) about marriage. The children were given a template to support them to plan their factsheet.

Lesson 7

In this lesson the children used their planning sheets to write their factsheet on marriage.

CRITICAL QUESTIONS

+ What challenges might schools experience in the implementation of this scheme of work?

+ How might schools overcome these challenges?

+ How might the school involve religious leaders in the delivery of some aspects of this unit; for example, the lesson on marriage?

✛ Do you think the above sequence of lessons is logical? Is there anything missing from the unit? Is there anything you would change? What might you add to the scheme of work?

MEETING THE NEEDS OF LOOKED-AFTER CHILDREN

Children end up living in care for a variety of reasons. Some children may have been removed from their parents because of safeguarding concerns. Some parents may have died and some parents may be in prison. These are just some of the reasons why children may end up living in care.

Supporting children to improve their behaviour, confidence and self worth will help them to develop positive relationships with adults and peers. Children who are living in care will need plenty of praise, support and encouragement to boost their self worth. If they have not established secure attachments with a key individual in their lives, their relationship with their teacher at school needs to be positive and based on mutual trust and respect. Instilling within them a growth mindset and developing the skill of perseverance will support them to develop academically. This will improve their self esteem and this will support them to develop positive relationships with others.

Children living in care may find it difficult to establish secure, trusting relationships. There are various reasons for this, but one explanation is that they may not have established warm, trusting, nurturing relationships with people in their family. They may have been exploited, lied to and rejected by their parents and carers. These factors can make it difficult for children who are living in care to establish positive relationships with peers. In addition, if these children have experienced sexual abuse, they may have developed an advanced, but unhealthy, knowledge about sex. Teachers need to take into account these factors when planning the Relationships Education curriculum for children living in care. Although children living in care may not have previous experiences of positive relationships, a well-designed Relationships Education curriculum that addresses their specific needs can support them to establish effective future relationships.

Children living in care may need an individual programme of Relationships Education which is tailored to their needs. They may need to talk about their previous experiences before they can start to learn about positive and caring relationships. They may have established character traits which they have modelled from the people around them and they may need a personalised intervention to support them in developing confidence, self worth and appropriate behaviour.

CRITICAL QUESTIONS

+ What are the advantages and disadvantages of providing an individual programme of Relationships Education that is tailored to address the needs of children living in care?

+ What are the factors that might influence the capacity of looked-after children to establish positive relationships with others?

SUMMARY

This chapter has emphasised that children of the same age might be developmentally at different stages. It has therefore outlined the importance of ensuring that teaching methods consider children's different needs, particularly in relation to those with Special Educational Needs and Disabilities (SEND). It has highlighted the requirements of the statutory framework for Relationships Education in relation to these needs and it has explained the benefits of employing flexible modes of delivery. The chapter has also explained that some children may need a specific programme which is tailored to meet their needs and that some delivery might take place in small groups and some delivery might take place with the whole class. The relationship education needs of children with SEND have been discussed as well as the needs of those who identify as LGBT and those who are looked after. Case study material has been offered to illuminate effective practice and critical questions have been asked to support your reflection.

FURTHER READING OR SOURCES OF FURTHER INFORMATION

Glazzard, J and Stones, S (2019) *Supporting LGBTQ+ Inclusion in Primary Schools*. Leeds: Glazzard and Stones.

Martindale, D (2018) Supporting Looked After Children in Your School. *Secondary Education*. [online] Available at: www.sec-ed.co.uk/best-practice/supporting-looked-after-children-in-your-school/ (accessed 30 January 2020).

Office for Standards in Education, Children's Services and Skills (Ofsted) (2008) *Looked After Children: Good Practice in Schools*. Manchester: Ofsted.

✚ CONCLUSION

This book has provided an overview of the statutory framework for Relationships Education (DfE, 2019a). It has emphasised the importance of teaching children to develop caring friendships and respectful relationships. It has highlighted the importance of developing safe online relationships and the need to be a good digital citizen. It has emphasised the importance of children knowing about different types of identities and relationships, including LGBT relationships and same-sex marriage. In addition, this book has discussed the importance of children knowing how to look after their physical health and mental well-being.

There has been opposition to this framework. The requirement to teach children in primary schools about LGBT families and identities has been challenged by individuals and groups who feel that this is not age appropriate. This book has emphasised that schools play a critical role in educating children about diversity and in fostering inclusive values. We have argued that the term 'age appropriate' itself is controversial, given that many children will live in families that include LGBT parents and they may have siblings, cousins or aunties and uncles who identify as LGBT. Denying children access to a curriculum that promotes LGBT inclusion does not foster a sense of belonging for children who have families that are different to the majority of families. From the earliest possible age, children need to understand that LGBT identities and relationships are valid in British law and should be respected. This prepares children for life in modern Britain. In the implementation of this curriculum, schools must consult with parents. However, parents have no right to veto this curriculum and they have no legal right to withdraw their children from Relationships Education. If schools do not implement this guidance, this will allow prejudice to prevail. Schools play a crucial role in challenging prejudice and in helping children to foster inclusive attitudes and values. If schools fail to address this due to fear of parental backlash then they are letting children down.

Through the physical health and well-being curriculum which forms part of the statutory framework, schools also must address a range of controversial topics that may cause conflict with parental values. These topics include drug and alcohol abuse, smoking, healthy eating, physical exercise, teeth hygiene, social media use and online gaming. Although children may be exposed to these at home, it is important that children understand that neglecting to look after one's physical and mental well-being can be unhealthy and lead to illness. Schools should address this sensitively and ensure that children do not feel stigmatised because of the choices that their family members make.

The Relationships Education guidance offers hope for a brighter future. It promotes the values of respect and care and it highlights the need for healthy lifestyles. It is a powerful curriculum which aims to eradi-cate prejudice, discrimination and stigma. It reflects the realities of life in modern Britain. It should support children to lead long, healthy and active lives as full members of the communities in which they live. It supports the development of positive character virtues which will enable children to form effective relationships and achieve long-term outcomes.

✚ REFERENCES

Catholic Education Service (2018)
Made in God's Image: Challenging Homophobic and Biphobic Bullying in Catholic Schools. London: St Mary's University.

Chanfreau, J, Tanner, E, Callanan, M, Laing, K, Skipp, A and Todd, L (2016)
Out of School Activities During Primary School and KS2 Attainment, Centre for Longitudinal Studies, Working paper 2016/1. London: Institute of Education, University College London.

Church of England Education Service (2017)
Valuing All God's Children: Guidance for Church of England Schools on Challenging Homophobic, Biphobic and Transphobic Bullying. London: Church of England Education Service.

Department for Education (DfE) (2013)
The National Curriculum in England: Key Stages 1 and 2 Framework Document. London: DfE.

Department for Education (DfE) (2019a)
Relationships Education, Relationships and Sex Education (RSE) and Health Education: Statutory Guidance for Governing Bodies, Proprietors, Head Teachers, Principals, Senior Leadership Teams, Teachers. London: DfE.

Department for Education (DfE) (2019b)
Character Education: Framework Guidance. London: DfE.

Durlak, J A, Weissberg, R P, Dymnicki, A B, Taylor, R D and Schellinger, K B (2011)
The Impact of Enhancing Students' Social and Emotional Learning: A Meta-Analysis of School-Based Universal Interventions. *Child Development*, 82: 405–32.

Equality Act (2010)

Protected Characteristics. [online] Available at: www.legislation.gov.uk/ukpga/
2010/15/pdfs/ukpga_20100015_en.pdf (accessed 16 December 2019).

Gegenfurtner, A and Gebhardt, M (2017)

Sexuality Education Including Lesbian, Gay, Bisexual, and Transgender (LGBT)
Issues in Schools. *Educational Research Review*, 22(1): 215–22.

Glazzard, J and Mitchell, C (2018)

Social Media and Mental Health in Schools. St Albans: Critical Publishing.

Glazzard, J and Stones, S (2019)

Supporting LGBTQ+ Inclusion in Primary Schools. Leeds: Glazzard and Stones.

Gutman, L M and Schoon, I (2013)

*The Impact of Non-Cognitive Skills on Outcomes for Young People: Literature
Review*. London: Education Endowment Foundation and Cabinet Office.

Marriage (Same Sex Couples) Act (2013)

[online] Available at: www.legislation.gov.uk/ukpga/2013/30/contents/
enacted (accessed 16 December 2019).

Mirvis, E (2018)

The Wellbeing of LGBT+ Pupils: A Guide for Orthodox Jewish Schools. [online]
Available at: https://chiefrabbi.org/wp-content/uploads/2018/09/The-
Wellbeing-of-LGBT-Pupils-A-Guide-for-Orthodox-Jewish-Schools.pdf (accessed
30 January 2020).

Moffitt, T E, Arseneault, L, Belsky, D, Dickson, N, Hancox, R J, Harrington, H and Caspi, A (2011)

A Gradient of Childhood Self-Control Predicts Health, Wealth, and Public
Safety. *Proceedings of the National Academy of Sciences*, 108(7): 2693–98

OECD (2015)

Skills for Social Progress: The Power of Social and Emotional Skills. Paris: OECD
Skills Studies, OECD Publishing.

Office for Standards in Education, Children's Services and Skills (Ofsted) (2019)

Education Inspection Framework. Manchester: Ofsted.

Taylor, R D, Oberle, E, Durlak, J A and Weissberg, R P (2017)
Promoting Positive Youth Development Through School-Based Social and
Emotional Learning Interventions: A Meta-Analysis of Follow-Up Effects. *Child
Development*, 88(4): 1156–71.

Walker, M, Sims, D and Kettlewell, K (2017)
Case Study Report: Leading Character Education in Schools. Slough: National
Foundation for Educational Research.

✚ INDEX